KARSH. OTTAWA

karen

karen

The Karen Magnussen Story

KAREN MAGNUSSEN
JEFF CROSS

Collier-Macmillan Canada, Ltd.

Cover: Original painting by Vancouver artist Geoffrey Traunter, especially commissioned by the Prudential Insurance Company of America for its 'Great Moments in Canadian Sport' collection.

Design: William Fox/Associates

Library of Congress Catalog Card Number: 73-16939
SBN: 02.975690.1

Collier-Macmillan Canada, Ltd.
1125B Leslie Street
Don Mills, Ontario

Macmillan Publishing Co., Inc.
New York

PRINTED AND BOUND IN CANADA
1 2 3 4 5   77 76 75 74 73

contents

karen

PROLOGUE

The last time – how could I forget – I'd played porter for her, lugging two damned great carry-alls through that empty arena in Bratislava. Skates – two, three pairs – costumes, makeup, and a couple of heavy-as-lead but absolutely price-less Czech crystal vases. Back in the Magnussen home in North Vancouver, I immediately spotted those vases on the sideboard.

Karen giggled when I noticed them. "Remem-ber? We nearly missed the last bus back to the hotel because they were so heavy."

That had been the first week in March. Now it was an early summer morning. The vases were acting as temporary bookends for hundreds of congratulatory letters and telegrams, and the girl who had earned them was curled up in an easy chair across from me, looking small and sleepy, not at all like the dazzling dynamo who had captured the figure skating championship of the world just a few weeks before.

Now she was the toast of all Canada, the recipient of countless gifts and honors, her name on the lips of sports enthusiasts throughout the world, her future financially secure, bright and beckoning.

As always, she was warm, friendly, good-natured. But quiet, content here in the comfortable surroundings of her family home, not quite awake after all those late nights, celebrations, receptions, non-stop telephone calls from admirers and friends.

"That's Jason," she murmured, as a kitten leaped from nowhere onto my lap. "He's crazy. But I guess he's like all cats. Just when you think he's yours, off he goes to someone else."

This was Karen Magnussen, the girl who had returned from Europe with the first world skating title ever won by anyone from Western Canada, whose five-foot-three, 115-pound shapely figure had appeared in more newspapers the past weeks than any Hollywood movie star. But she was still the same girl whose footsteps I had dogged for the past seven years – from inauspicious district championships at Prince George, deep in the interior of British Columbia, to Olympic Games triumphs in Japan and world championship successes in Europe and North America.

Other members of the Magnussen family appeared briefly, one by one, this morning. Her mother, Gloria, petite, blond, and dynamic, hollered from the kitchen that she'd be with us in a minute. Alf Magnussen, quiet, smiling, poked his balding head around the door, said "Hi," then excused himself to continue working on some new bathroom cupboards. Lori, eighteen, and Judy, fifteen, as blond as their sister, wandered in and out again – Lori wanting to borrow Karen's car, Judy checking on everyone's plans for the day.

The living room floor was layered with Gloria's scrapbooks – thick bound volumes, the memorabilia of a fifteen year career, from the time a little girl of six first laced on a pair of skates.

"I guess Mom's really got her work cut out now," smiled Karen, glancing down at the pile of newspaper and magazine clippings waiting to be added to the file. "That sure has been a lot of work. But then, it covers such a long time." Her blue eyes were reflective, as she gazed out of the picture window across the well-kept sunlit garden.

"You know, it's going to be very strange for a while, not having to get up at the crack of dawn and drive down to the club to practice. Seems like I've been doing that all my life . . ."

Has it all been worthwhile? The heartaches, the triumphs and the despair, the endless hours of practice, the pain and the frustration?

Karen looked thoughtful. "Sometimes I've wondered about it all," she said, in that slow, little-girl way she has of talking. "I've asked myself whether it was really what I wanted to do. But when I look back over the years, then think about how it all came together for me in Bratislava – there really isn't any question to answer."

1

FINAL ACT OF A LONG DRAMA

Sure, you've got to expect to sacrifice a lot if you hope to reach a goal. But, really, it's not that much of a sacrifice when you consider the satisfaction you feel after the work is done.

Thursday, the first day of March 1973, was much like any other day in Bratislava, the somber, ancient capital of Slovakia. It was chilly. Not cold enough to keep its hardy citizens indoors, but biting enough to discourage rendezvous in Hviezdoslavovo, the pleasant, tree-lined square near the main hotels.

People scurried off the crowded, single-deck tramcars, intent on their own business. Most appeared preoccupied with the routine mechanics of a humdrum existence.

Citizens queued stoically at outdoor booths offering goods currently in short supply. That day it was oranges. Some lined up at store counters, exchanging their hard-earned koruny for a much more meager variety of goods than could be bought in glittering Vienna, a mere thirty-five miles away across the East-West border. No shortage of money, apparently, and the same universal urge to splurge, in spite of sparse selection.

Life in Bratislava, where one gray day follows the next in drab monotony, seems to have left its mark on the 300,000 inhabitants. To the visitor, faces on the street show calm, almost stolid acceptance of a dreary, though not unpalatable routine.

Perhaps the chill March weather pointed up the flat feeling. As evening approached, that Thursday, a brisk wind whipped along Razusovo, the street that parallels the softly swirling River Danube.

A crowd in topcoats, fur hats, and gloves milled around the entrance to Zimny Stadium, the imposing ice arena on the fringe of the city. Busy uniformed attendants directed early arrivals to the right entrances, while constantly clearing a path through the good-natured throng for officials, contestants, newspapermen, and other visitors, who arrived in a steady stream of buses from their downtown bases at the Carlton, Devin, and Kyjev Hotels.

The World Figure Skating championships of 1973 had brought a mood of unusual animation to Bratislava. It was most in evidence here at the stadium. But it was just as noticeable wherever the young skaters from twenty-two countries congregated. Scores of intrigued citizens spent hours clustered in groups outside the three main hotels, just watching the comings and goings of the visitors, happy just to be on the fringe of all the excitement generated by this glamorous international sporting event. (Very young Bratislavans, however, had found their own fascination – the automatic glass doors at the entrance to the ultramodern Kyjev Hotel, which had been barely completed in time to house newspaper, radio, and television personnel from around the world. Harassed doormen spent fruitless hours chasing away impish youngsters who persistently jumped on the pressure pads that opened the doors.)

It was the third day of the skating championships. But that evening Zimny Stadium was charged with an electricity unlike anything witnessed on the two previous days of competition. Tonight the crowd waited for the crowning of the skating world's new queen.

Figure skating gives boys and girls an equal chance to show their talents. Male competitors may demonstrate their own athletic skills. But, ever since the era of Sonja Henie, it has been the girls who have captured the imagination of the crowds. So the battle for the ladies' crown in the 1973 world championships already had a built-in attraction, long before national competition around the world had eliminated hundreds of hopeful aspirants and narrowed the field to twenty-eight young women.

But there was more to this single event than merely the annual competition between the best skaters in the world. All of the 11,000 spectators crowded into the brightly lit arena, and surely most of the millions watching on television throughout the world, were aware that, for two of the girls, there was more at stake than just a skating contest.

Karen Magnussen, twenty-year-old Canadian champion from North Vancouver, Britsh Columbia, was certainly aware of it. So was Janet Lynn, the nineteen-year-old United States' champion from Rockford, Illinois. For years, competition in the women's world championship had pointed to this day. For many skating observers, the preceding years had been but a prelude. This was the finale. Ever since the 1968 Winter Olympics in Grenoble, France, when the pair had met for the first time in international competition, it had been obvious that the day would come when direct confrontation for the biggest prize of all would be inevitable. The stage, certainly, had been well set.

Only once in their many competitive meetings since the '68 Olympics had the American girl finished ahead of the Canadian. And that victory, at the 1969 North American championships in Oakland, California, had been so highly controversial that within three years the much-criticized North American event was scrapped by its two member-nations. The 1971 North American championships at Peterborough, Ontario, were the last of the series. And, fittingly, they provided a showcase for Karen, who swept to one of the most decisive triumphs of her career. But for the two North American rivals Oakland and Peterborough were only two of the stops along the route to the top.

Alike in appearance – blond, engaging, and extremely attractive – the two girls presented markedly different skating styles: Janet, almost ethereal, came across to the public as an effortless, graceful performer, but with a technical merit debated endlessly by experts; Karen seemed the epitome of determination and courage, the super-athlete whose will to win never detracted from her complete femininity.

Trixi Schuba, the big Austrian girl whose penchant for school figures had propelled her to the world title in 1971 and 1972 and the Olympic crown in Sapporo, Japan, also in 1972, had departed from the amateur scene for the lucrative world of ice-show-business. Karen, silver medalist behind Miss Schuba at both the Winter Olympics and the '72 world championships in Calgary, Alberta, obviously was the ranking contender for the world title. Equally obviously, Janet, who had won the bronze medal in both 1972 events, was the one most likely to challenge.

The history of international figure-skating competition suggested a logical victory for the Canadian girl. For many years, natural progression had been the accepted format. The champion retired and everyone moved up a notch, with minor variations on the theme. This year, however, for the first time there was a flaw in the progression concept. No longer could anyone expect automatic advancement when those at the top retired.

In its desire to parade a more attractive package for the rapidly growing numbers of enthusiasts around the world and the new millions of intrigued television watchers, the International Skating Union in Switzerland had ordered a new format for 1973. Instead of allocating marks on the basis of 50 per cent for school figures and 50 per cent for the free-skating program, an entirely new method of marking would come into effect. Now competitors would be required to skate only three figures, instead of the previous six. These would count for 40 per cent of the total marks.

Then, on another day, skaters would be required to perform a newly devised "short, compulsory free-skating program," a two-minute (or shorter) program incorporating six specific elements selected by the ISU. This new program would count for 20 per cent of total marks, with the remaining 40 per cent allocated for the final long free-skating program, a four-minute session in which skaters have virtually complete freedom to show off their talents.

This sweeping change in world competition standards would be introduced in Bratislava. From here on, the new formula would be the indicator of a skater's talent. No longer would it be possible to gloss over a deficiency in any particular phase of the sport by a super-abundance of talent in another. To win, you had to do it all – and do it all better than anyone else. The often dreary patterns of school figures, basically variations of figure eights on specified edges of the skate blade, would still hold a degree of importance, but one could not now expect to win a championship on the strength of figures alone, as had often been the case in the past, particularly in 1972.

How this new format would affect the chances of the two main candidates for the ladies' world championship had been the subject of long discussion ever since the ISU decision. The formidable American propaganda machine, led by television commentator and former world champion Dick Button, had gleefully – and incessantly – forecast victory for Janet, claiming she was the superior free-skater and thus would benefit more from the new formula.

This campaign had achieved some measure of success. In many published and televised accounts of the pre-championship scene, Karen's name was missing. The official brochure of the Czechoslovak organizing committee, for instance, suggested that the winner would emerge from the trio of Janet Lynn, Sonja Morgenstern of East Germany, and Christine Errath of East Germany. No mention of Magnussen. (The same brochure also suggested, as a twosome to watch in the pairs' event, Britain's Michael Hutchinson and Jayne Torville, who were not even entered. So perhaps there was a clue to the value of that assessment.)

Four weeks earlier, American television coverage of the U.S. national championships had veered away from the competition at Bloomington, Minnesota, just long enough to explain to viewers that Janet's main opposition in the forth-coming world championships could be expected from Canadian champion Karen Magnussen – then proceeded to show a tiny fragment of film from the Canadian championships, a clip that showed Karen falling on an intended jump.

The innuendo resulted in many messages of apology to the Magnussen home from embarrassed Americans, including Mrs. Doris Fleming, mother of former world champion Peggy Fleming. Its effect on Karen?

"That kind of thing makes me want to fight harder," she said. "If it was intended to psych me out, it had just the opposite effect." The effect was to push Karen Magnussen to her greatest triumph, to set the seal on a brilliant and dynamic career of competitive skating.

But to describe that triumph in detail here would be to rob the reader of the heart-warming story of a Canadian girl who dreamed of sitting on top of the world, and made the dream come true.

2

A PAIR OF FIVE DOLLAR SKATES

"She is a very straight little girl, good muscular control and can relax well. She plays and works well with others, but she is a little inclined to want to lead, rather than follow. . . ."

(1957 Kindergarten report on Karen Diane Magnussen, aged five.)

She was a chubby six-year-old wearing five-dollar second-hand skates the first time she ever teetered out on the ice. It was one of the Saturday afternoon public skating sessions at Vancouver's Kerrisdale Arena, and Karen and her best friend, Cathy Lee Irwin, had gone with their mothers.

Nobody, least of all Gloria Magnussen or Lee Irwin, could have suspected what the next fifteen years would bring – that one of those two little blond girls would be the champion of the world, the other right behind her as runner-up for the championship of Canada. But anybody could tell, just from their shouts of delight as they tumbled and fumbled their way around the rink that day, that they found it fun, and before the afternoon was over their mothers had arranged for their memberships in the Kerrisdale Skating Club. Dr.

Hellmut May was their first coach. An Austrian Olympic skater, he had come to Canada from his native Vienna in 1954; he took over as head professional at the Kerrisdale Club a year later.

He had been only fourteen when he was selected as a member of the Austrian team sent to compete in the Winter Olympics of 1936 in Garmisch-Partenkirchen, Germany, and the subsequent world championships in Paris. (That was the year, incidentally, that another skater, the comely Norwegian Sonja Henie, was leaving the world of competitive skating for the glossier world of show business, to parlay her ten consecutive world titles and three Olympic gold medals into the most lucrative motion picture career of her era.) May himself never scaled such heights, though he touched the fringe, winning selection to three Olympic teams. One of his last attempts for international honors was the 1947 world championships in Stockholm, when for the first time North American skating power came to the fore with the victory of Canada's Barbara Ann Scott, first skater from this continent to win a world title.

May had retired from competitive skating the following year, the year that Dick Button of the United States won his first world championship. After a seven-year career with the famed Vienna Ice Revue, the tall, articulate Austrian decided to stake his dual talents – on the ice and in the business world (a Ph.D. in Economics from the University of Vienna) – on a future in North

America. It was a decision that led him, in 1955, to Vancouver, to Kerrisdale Arena, and to Karen Magnussen.

In the 1950's artificial ice surfaces were scarce in the Greater Vancouver area. In North Vancouver, on the other side of the harbor, only the posh Capilano Winter Club boasted a rink. Casual skaters had to make the tiresome journey into Vancouver to find available ice.

Coach May quickly had a full register of skating students at Kerrisdale – so many that he couldn't accommodate the Magnussens and the Irwins when they requested private lessons for their two little girls. Instead Karen and Cathy Lee went into group lessons to learn the basics – how to stand up on skates, how to skate on one foot, and even how to attempt crossovers.

But within a few weeks, both youngsters had been worked into the individual coaching schedule of Hellmut May. So it was this quiet, gentle Austrian who laid the foundations for the triumphs to come. From here on, it was practice, practice, practice. And, like all the others, Karen went through the mill.

The complex and complicated structure of figure skating is laid down in minute detail and constantly being revised by national and international authorities. The code is followed strictly in Canada, possibly more than in any other country. The rule book is law, and liberties with its sanctity are forbidden. More than one world-class skater has despaired of this inflexibility. "I know the Canadian officials are going by the book, but how can I compete against skaters from other countries, when I'm barred from doing things that they actually get credit for?"

In Canada the name of the game is strict observance of the rules – for example:

A candidate, to be eligible for a test, must have passed all of the preceding tests in the same category. . . .

A candidate is not permitted to receive instruction or coaching from the time he is called by the referee to skate his performance until its completion – the referee may disqualify a candidate who violates this rule and may bar from the rink any person who disregards it. . . .

To pass a test, a candidate must receive the minimum mark from two of the three judges, with an average of the three judges' marks at least equal to the minimum mark. . . .

And there are many, many more. The official rule book of the Canadian Figure Skating Association, for example, comprises 194 pages of type.

Figure tests range from Preliminary Test through First (Bronze) Test, Second, Third, Fourth (Silver), Fifth, Sixth, and Seventh to the Eighth or Gold Test. Free-skating is handled separately until the Sixth Test stage.

The Preliminary Test requires "skating on forward outside and inside edges and backward outside and inside edges; the first two figures – forward outside eight and forward inside eight; and a waltz eight."

Maximum points for the Preliminary Test are 18.0. The minimum mark is 2.7, the passing total is 9.0 and the average mark 3.0. And the rule book sternly admonishes: "The candidate must show substantial steadiness and shall be failed for lack of ability to skate clean edges on a flexible and bended knee." Karen Magnussen took her Preliminary Test in 1959. She passed it comfortably.

From that day onwards, progress was steady, if unspectacular. There was not much to suggest that the cuddly little girl was different from dozens of other beginners, although the first signs of natural ability were not long in emerging. As Hellmut May recalls:

"She had none of the fragility, for instance, of her friend Cathy Lee. Karen was a cute little youngster, strong, graceful, and talented, whereas Cathy was more artistic. Most of all, I remember Karen's strong determination and always happy disposition.

"One day during practice, Karen became confused over which toe pick to use in landing a jump I was teaching her to do in both directions. She burst into tears because it seemed so difficult for her to master. I thought perhaps I had overdone it a little, but then, she seemed so talented by this time that sometimes I got carried away and thought she should be able to do everything I asked." Karen, meanwhile, was also enrolled in the ballet classes conducted by Dr. May's wife, Doris, a graduate of the Vienna Academy of Dance, and here again Karen revealed the natural grace she had shown on the ice.

"Right from the start she mastered the fundamentals of skating," says Dr. May, "and she quickly proved to be one of the few gifted persons out of the hundreds who skated at the club. This is normal, in my experience. There are very few you can evaluate as gifted, or even promising enough to warrant continuing with lessons. Most of the kids you can rule out right away because you can see they just don't have the potential.

"This session in 1958 produced an extremely good crop of skaters. From that same class, on the same sheet of ice, at the same time, came the three girls who were to become one-two-three in the country, and represent Canada at the 1972 Olympic Games in Sapporo, Japan – Karen, Ruth Hutchinson and Cathy Lee Irwin. I think that must be unique in skating; certainly it is in Canada.

"But, in addition to being capable, athletic, and graceful, Karen was also a very normal girl. She was never difficult, but always easy to teach, nice to get along with in every way, a real nice kid. And she has stayed that way."

For the summer of 1959, with tuition fees paid by her grandmother, Karen moved with Dr. May to a special summer school at North Vancouver's Capilano Winter Club, where she spent the entire session working on her Preliminary Test. "The Magnussens couldn't understand why this should take so long," recalls May. "But many years later Mrs. Magnussen told me she had come to realize how necessary it had been, and that Karen herself was very grateful for it, because it gave her the sound basis to work from."

Success in the Preliminary Test was the competitive beginning for Karen. But the real highlight of those formative sessions was to come in the following winter season back at Kerrisdale, a season climaxed for members of the juvenile class by a miniature free-skating competition, in which the youngsters performed a one-and-a-half minute program of their own devising. Right there Karen Magnussen's brilliant competitive fire showed its first spark. And today a small silver trophy still occupies a proud place among the glittering array of cups, medals, badges, ribbons, and other mementos of a fabulous career – a small trophy for the winner of Kerrisdale Skating Club's special juvenile free-skating competition for 1959-60, Miss Karen Magnussen – aged seven.

3

JUST ONE OF THE FAMILY

Karen cried. Gloria Magnussen cried.
Alf Magnussen, the silent partner of Team
Magnussen over the years, made a brief and
impressive thank-you speech and choked a little
– admitting, "I get a little emotional, too."

"Team Magnussen" the sportswriters labeled them. And a team they truly were – Karen, her mother, and her coach, Linda Brauckmann. Together they made it to the top of the world. It couldn't have been done any other way. A skater could never make it to world class just on talent and burning desire alone. Somebody has to be around to bolster that desire when it falters. Someone must be ready with sound counsel when the whole future may hang on a decision taken at a critical moment.

Someone has to be able to "run interference" when an unsophisticated youngster meets up with off-ice intrigue and politics for the first time. And there has to be a comforting shoulder to lean on, even to cry on, whenever the skater's confidence deserts her.

Karen has been one of the lucky ones. Hers has been a close-knit, happy family, behind her all the way. Oldest of the three Magnussen sisters

(Lori is three years younger, Judy three years younger than Lori), Karen is an amalgam of her parents. The determination, drive, and complete dedication to the job at hand she inherited from her mother. Her thoughtfulness, even temper, and sunny disposition were gifts from her father. And in the tough, demanding years that marked her climb to the peak of the skating world, Karen has needed all those virtues.

"Gloria was determined, right from the beginning, to take Karen to the top," said one of her coaches. In that respect only, Gloria Magnussen has been a "Skating Mother." Skating Mothers are legion, the bane of every coach's existence. They throw their hands at the mention of the term, recounting tales of over-possessive, demanding, strident-voiced females who bulldoze their daughters into prominence on the ice. Many of the world's top skaters have been known as much for the outrageous antics and opinions of their mothers as for their own skills on the blades.

Gloria has exhibited none of the obstreperous traits of the prototype, but she has certainly been zealous in channeling all her efforts toward furthering her daughter's career.

"Gloria was lucky to have had such a piece of putty to mold," said former coach Edy Rada. But he gave her top marks for complete dedication: "Without her mother, Karen would never have made it."

Always, she's been there to take care of the in-fighting, to become, in almost every sense of the word, a manager. First there were car pools to be organized with other mothers. Then, as successes mounted, she had to be packed and ready to accompany her daughter, as invitations poured in from all over the world for personal appearances and press, radio, and television interviews. The replies to letters from skating enthusiasts and fans near and far, the every-day details constantly cropping up – Gloria handled all these things.

Alf Magnussen, a quiet, unassuming realtor who came out to Canada as a boy from his native Norway, has stayed on the sidelines, yet has always been regarded by his family as the head of the household, in the traditional European manner. (Gloria's ancestry, incidentally, is Swedish.)

When Team Magnussen was away in London, Moscow, Tokyo, or any of the scores of cities throughout the world that Karen has visited, Alf Magnussen stayed home with Lori and Judy. Only on special occasions did he venture from home to watch his oldest daughter's skating successes. For the rest he chose the selfless responsibility of "minding the store," patiently awaiting the inevitable long-distance phone call that followed every championship, every personal appearance tour, every out-of-town engagement.

The bond between Karen and her father is real, and one of deep mutual affection. In many a reflective moment away from home she's said, "I wish my Dad could be here." More than one press or television interview following a championship victory has been held up, or interrupted, when that all-important call to North Vancouver was put through.

And always there were letters back and forth. Like this one from Alf to Gloria and Karen:

Hello, my darlings:

You both have made us very proud again. And I have a hunch there is more to come. The lonelies kind of sneaked up on us just after you left. I guess we'll never get used to being without you, and the depressing part is that it is just starting.

Things are going as well as can be expected around here. Lori and Judy at times are the spirit of cooperation, but then there are those other times!

This morning Judy's week of packing came to its conclusion and she headed off to Paradise Valley. I believe that Paradise is right here, because since she left Lori has dug in and taken the dishes and pots *and the stove* under her wing. She had dinner ready at five o'clock when I got home – fried chicken, boiled potatoes and beans, of all things. She now wants to know my schedule so dinner can be planned ahead.

I'm slowly but steadily forging ahead with the rec. room so this week should see the valance and the drop-ceiling over the bar finished. We'll keep you posted between competitions.

There are lots of nice things being said about you in the papers, and believe me, there's no end of moral support. More people have stopped me on the street and at the club to offer congratulations and wish you success.

Gloria and Karen, we already miss you a whole bunch, so stay away only as long as you have to, and don't worry. Everything is fine, as we hope it is with you.

All our (my) love,
Alf.

Fourteen of Karen's twenty-one years have been spent, first by coincidence, later by design, on reaching a goal. And to a large degree this has become the pivot on which the life of the family centered. Yet Karen was never allowed to develop any ideas about being "different" from other girls her age, or from her sisters.

"We never let her become a prima donna," says Alf, "not that I think she would have, anyway. But she did whatever work had to be done around the house. She has always had to do her share.

"I wouldn't want to give the impression she was any kind of saint. She was like any other girl her age. But I honestly can't recall any occasion when she took off on any kind of 'star' kick. And I think that was because she had to work so hard for everything she got. You know, she hasn't always won. There were lots of times when it was rough, really rough. Every once in a while she would get slapped down. And I think it was those times that made her the kind of person she is."

The other Scandinavian-blond Magnussen sisters were not sacrificed on the altar of Karen's skating successes. Both had their chance to try for similar careers. Both were on skates at an early age. Both have been the victims of such well-meant rubs as, "Well, are you going to be as good a skater as your sister?" And both have smiled politely, secretly making personal vows to do anything but skate.

The decisions were their own, made without rancor, without any parental attempts to either persuade or dissuade. Both girls are immensely proud of their sister's success, happy to share in the moments of triumph, equally willing to be there at times of gloom and despondency.

To them both, perhaps particularly to Lori, Karen is not just a famous international sports figure. She's more an older sister with whom to share girlish confidences.

Following her world championship victory in Bratislava and the aftermath of the subsequent European tour, the civic and government receptions and the triumphant return home, Karen had the opportunity of a holiday on the French Riviera – for two. The companion she chose was sister Lori, and for both it was a highlight. Because, except for trips taken by Karen and Gloria in connection with competitions, the Magnussens have never felt financially able to join the jet set.

The years have proved that it's almost impossible to groom and develop a skater, no matter how talented, without spending a lot of money. In later years the Magnussens were helped by a few grants, but initially they had to foot the expenses alone. Professional tuition doesn't come cheap. And the higher a skater reaches in competition, the more expensive it becomes, roughly $1,000 a year in the final stages.

Equipment cuts into the budget. Karen's boots are hand-made, costing about $100 a pair. Blades must be perfect. In her final seasons of competitive skating, Karen's two sets of blades – one for figures, one for free-skating – came to $100 a pair. Skating dresses are tremendously important, must be functional as well as attractive, styled to reflect the individuality and personality of the girl. Remember that half of the total mark awarded a skater in competition is based on that rather nebulous factor known as "artistic impression." And, although in theory a skater's wardrobe should have no effect on a judge's mark, it can't help but have a bearing on the overall artistic impression she makes during her performance. So specially designed costumes are a must. Some girls will have a wardrobe of thirty or forty. Karen settled for a few simple dresses, made first by her mother, latterly by dressmaker friends of the family.

There are expenses involved in the preparation of the music for a skater's programs. Reproduction must be first-rate. Cutting and splicing and recording must be done professionally, and costs can run as high as fifty dollars for a complete record. Karen's record-carrying case was made by her father; otherwise it too would have added to the expense.

Answering the thousands of fan letters and sending out autographed pictures represent a real financial outlay. Not too many requests come accompanied by stamped, self-addressed envelopes.

One of the costliest items is ice-time, but any skater fighting for the championship of the world, or even a small part of the world, simply must have it. And since her ultimate perfection demands hours of total concentration, she mustn't be distracted by other skaters working out at the same time. That means the rink must be rented for her alone – at a cost of $10 to $15 an hour.

When a skater goes into top-level competition, many of the championships are held thousands of miles from home. Air fares, hotel accommodation, and meals figure high on the expense sheet, somewhere in the neighborhood of $3,000 to $4,000 a year. The coach must go along to watch every move, to advise and correct, and the tab for this is picked up by the skater or her family. What has it cost to produce a world champion? Of all the questions asked the Magnussens, that one is the most common. They're reluctant to answer.

Alf Magnussen says only, "We've never counted the cost. There was a time when we had to decide whether it was practical, even whether it was possible, to embark on such an ambitious venture. The big decision really was made in 1965 when Karen won the B.C. Coast and B.C. Section championships, then went on to win the junior Canadian title in Calgary. That was when Karen realized – in fact we were told by people who would know – that she had this potential. So we all had to sit down and figure the odds.

"Quite frankly we were getting to the point where a decision simply had to be made. Costs were getting pretty severe, and we had the other two girls to consider. There could be no question of abandoning them.

"It took a lot of soul-searching, and we all had some misgivings, but we got together, talked it over, and decided that Karen would go ahead, into it totally. A decision had to be made, and we made it."

And what has been the cost of that decision? Even now Alf finds it hard to assess in terms of cold, hard cash. There was some help from the Canadian Figure Skating Association's Bursary Fund (a project that becomes increasingly worthwhile as Canada produces a growing number of potential champions), and other private sources.

But it takes no mathematical genius to estimate that the cost of transforming Karen Magnussen, from a six-year old with a pair of five-dollar skates, into Karen Magnussen, champion of the world, has run into approximately $50,000.

4

AN INTRODUCTION TO DISCIPLINE

*Today a skater has to have it all. If you don't,
there's always someone else ready to take over.
And Karen had it all.*
Hellmut May

It took three skilled technicians to produce the
Magnussen phenomenon. Though others had a
hand in it – specialists in figures, in dancing, in
athletics – Karen had only three coaches during
her career: Hellmut May, with whom she began,
Edy Rada, who was in charge during the formative years, and Linda Brauckmann, who put
it all together. These three widely disparate personalities transformed Karen from a six-year-old
beginner into the champion of the world, and she
is quick to acknowledge the debt she owes to
each.

"From Dr. May I received the groundwork
and, perhaps most of all, the ability to really enjoy what I was doing. From Mr. Rada I learned
about discipline, and what hard work was all
about. And in Mrs. Brauckmann I found a coach,
a counsellor, and companion all in one – a won-

derful person who became my pro and also my friend."

Karen's progress from May to Rada in 1960 was mainly an economic move. The North Shore Winter Club, which was to produce many skating champions in future years, had just been built in North Vancouver, not far from the Magnussen home on Thorncliffe Drive. Kerrisdale, ten miles further away, involved tedious trips across the Lions' Gate toll-bridge and through downtown Vancouver, often in heavy traffic, sometimes in miserable weather.

The Magnussens were among the first Winter Club members, even before the building was properly completed. Skaters had to use a boarded-off section of the curling rink. Edy Rada, a stocky, sandy-haired Viennese, was the first regular figure-skating coach at the club. And he brought impressive credentials to the job.

Because of the turmoil in Europe during his youth, Rada found himself in some strange situations. His father was a Czech national, but Edy was born in Vienna. During the Second World War, his nationality necessarily changed to German, but after the war he once again became an Austrian.

Skating competition in Europe at that time was on an "open" basis. One did not have to be a native of a particular country to enter its championship. So Edy's scrapbook contains some intriguing items. He was, at various times, the champion of Germany, Switzerland, and Poland.

He was Austrian champion for ten consecutive years, from 1939 to 1949, and he also won the junior championships of Germany, Switzerland, and Austria.

His international career suffered during the war, but in 1948 he placed third in the European championships. The competition that year, won by Dick Button of the United States, marked the last time non-Europeans were allowed to compete for the European title.

In 1949 Rada became European champion and placed third in the world championship won by Button. Then he turned pro and spent an unhappy year touring North America with the Ice Capades company ("I didn't like show business") before turning to coaching. Two winters in Hamilton, Ontario, a year back in Vienna, seven years at the Vancouver Skating Club – then the offer of the head professional's job at North Shore. Rada took over his new duties in September 1960, and before that month was out he had added the name of Karen Magnussen to his list of pupils.

"She had already passed her first test, and was working on her second when she came to me. She was a little chubby girl compared to her friend Cathy Lee Irwin, who was sort of skinny. They were both cute youngsters. Both had talent, sure – but, at eight years of age, who can tell?

"Karen was, I suppose, better than anyone else we had at North Shore, but then we didn't have very much, except, of course, Cathy Lee, Cynthia

Titcombe – who was a bit older – and one or two others. But Karen developed very well in the next four years, and at the end of that time there was no question of her potential."

Discipline undoubtedly played a big part in that development. For Rada was, above all else, a strict disciplinarian. Blunt, outspoken, fiercely intolerant of any sign of slackness among his pupils, Rada expected every student to adopt his code.

"If I told a pupil to be on the ice for patch at five o'clock, I expected that pupil to be there at five o'clock. If not, unless there was a good excuse, there'd be a penalty of twenty-five *pliés*. Sometimes they called me 'Hitler' or 'Gestapo,' though I think on the whole the discipline was appreciated by the children and their parents.

"Mind you, parents can be a problem – they instinctively take the part of the child rather than the pro. I remember one day I was pointing out some faults to Karen. Mrs. Magnussen became quite indignant and asked me if I couldn't say anything nice. I said, 'Yes, I think she is very talented, but after all, I am here to criticize your daughter, not to admire her.' "

Stern taskmaster or no, Rada got results. In 1964 the five girls who battled it out for the B.C. Sectional championships were all his pupils. But he also ran into problems.

"I found I had to ease up on the strict discipline, because some of the kids didn't like it and wanted to switch to another pro.

"But, with Karen, I believe it helped in the beginning, especially in the early test figures. She didn't pass all her tests first time around. But she was easy to teach. She had such a good imagination. You could negotiate with her. Karen was willing – you could mold her – whereas Cathy Lee was much more determined to have her own way."

So, in the sometimes tumultuous association with Edy Rada, Karen made her steady, if unspectacular way up the skating ladder. There were club and regional competitions entered; sometimes Karen won, sometimes Cathy Lee Irwin, or Cynthia Titcombe, Judy McLeod, or Lindsay Cowan. There was still no clear indication of the triumphs that lay ahead.

In the summer of 1964 Karen was working on her seventh test, a sort of skating milestone. She was on the fringe of national competition with several district and provincial successes to her credit. She had skated well in novice and juvenile competitions, winning some and placing high in others. There was a first-place finish in the 1961 B.C. Coast championships at Victoria; second to Cathy Lee Irwin in the 1962 B.C. Section novice championships at North Vancouver's Capilano Club; first place in the 1962 B.C. Coast junior championships at Vancouver's Kerrisdale; another victory in the 1963 B.C. Section junior championships at Prince George, and then a first senior triumph in the 1964 B.C. Coast championships at her own North Shore Club.

The excitement of victory, the sweet flush of success was now a motivating force for the youngster. It was thrilling, it was satisfying, it was good to win. Successes in these competitions brought more than medals and trophies. The word was out, around the growing number of skating clubs in British Columbia, that there was a lot of fine new free-skating talent at the North Shore Club. And invitations to the youngsters flowed in from all over, with requests for appearances at club shows and carnivals.

These were fun, and Karen loved them. They gave her a chance to demonstrate her skills as an entertainer as well as her skating proficiency. One of her contemporaries, now retired from competition, later put it this way: "In free-skating you have to be a bit of a show-off – and that's what Karen is, when she's on the ice. She likes to do something spectacular."

The carnivals and shows provided an even greater opportunity. Karen was always in demand for shows. In her first carnival, when she was very small, she was a "snowflake". She later became a doll, a clown, Peter Pan – whatever the show required. The annual shows at the North Shore Winter Club became one of the highlights of the winter season.

At this time the Eastern Canada "establishment" dominated the national skating competitions. Barbara Ann Scott, Barbara Wagner and Bob Paul, Donald Jackson, and Petra Burka won world championships from their home bases in

Toronto, Ottawa, and the surrounding areas. The West Coast was still a skating desert, though there were some signs that in Edy Rada's class of '64 lay hope for a change.

And it was then that Karen Magnussen met Linda Brauckmann.

5

TEACHER, CONFIDANTE – AND FRIEND

*The skater is the implement, the tool to work
with. It doesn't matter how good you are,
if you don't have the talent to work with, you're
nothing . . . the skaters are the ones that are
doing it. They're the ones that have the talent.*

*I don't need public recognition. I am what I am
– a skating teacher – and I do it fairly well,
and I've been fairly successful. For that, I'm
grateful – but I work damned hard at it.*

Linda Brauckmann is a tall blond streak of a
woman with Angie Dickinson legs, a journalist
husband, three children – and a world champion
pupil.

Her partnership with Karen Magnussen began
in the spring of 1964. Edy Rada had returned
to Austria for a holiday, and Linda, the other
senior pro at the North Shore Winter Club, took
over at Mrs. Magnussen's request.

The bond between Karen and Linda, which
has developed into something greater than a relationship between teacher and pupil had its be-
ginnings in Calgary, Alberta at the 1965 Canadian championships. Karen was entered in the

junior event, her first national competition.

"The figures were being done in a private club and I had to watch them from behind a glass panel," says Linda. "Karen was something like twentieth in the first figure and thirteenth in the next, and I was just fit to be tied. She had a sort of glassy look in her eyes. I think she was petrified.

"I believe that was the only time I was really thinking of myself. I thought of all the hours and hours I'd used up on figures in the last year with that girl, and I saw it all going up in smoke. This had no similarity to what I knew she could do. So when she came off the ice after one of the figures, I just gave her hell . . . I asked her just who did she think she was?

"All around us people were turning and staring. The tears welled up in her eyes, and she toddled off into the dressing room. I found out later she had gone to her mother and said: 'Oh, Mother, Mrs. Brauckmann's upsetting me and I can't do my figures.' And her mother replied, 'Karen, I think it's probably you who's upsetting Mrs. Brauckmann.' I think that said a lot for Gloria, that she had confidence that I had said the right thing.

"Anyway, Karen went out and won the next figure. She was second on the one after that, and won the last one. It pulled her all the way up from twentieth at the start to fifth at the end of figures. Then she did a fine job in the free-skating and with it won the overall junior championship.

Since then, we've never had anything but the greatest relationship."

"We have a lot of respect for each other," Karen says. "We can have very constructive arguments . . . she usually wins, but she lets me get my point across. She's interested in a skater as a person while some others are only interested in winning competitions, and the financial rewards."

That 1965 junior championship victory was the one that really launched Karen's competitive career. But even that had its memorable moments. In the midst of her free-skating performance, a program fell on to the ice. When a security guard hopped smartly over the boards to retrieve it, the audience yelled in alarm, fearful of a head-on collision. Later, when asked if she'd been thrown off stride by the sudden appearance of the man on the ice, Karen looked stunned. "What man?" she asked. She'd been so intent on the job at hand she hadn't even noticed.

Nevertheless it was a spectacular victory for the twelve-year-old youngster. In its report of the event, the Vancouver *Daily Province* said: "When the championships resume here this morning, the talk will still be of Miss Magnussen and her unbelievable comeback. It was without doubt the most amazing performance given by any skater in the 54 year history of these championships. When the free-skating began, Karen was in fifth place, 45.1 points behind the leader . . . but she skated her program to near perfection, landing six double jumps cleanly. It was Karen's seventh competition in six months, and she has won six of them."

It was then that Gloria and Alf Magnussen took the plunge and decided that Karen would have every chance to develop her obviously outstanding talents.

"I think her biggest thing was that she was a believer," says coach Linda. "You only had to tell her that she could do it, point out the pitfalls, and she'd follow directions exactly. She always did it when it counted. She has great inner strength. But that alone wouldn't have been enough, without the technical know-how to back it up.

"I always told her to skate for herself. If she was the best, she would win. It was as simple as that. We never planned to skate against somebody else — always for herself. And that's the way it has been."

(It's not much more than coincidence, since the North American skating fraternity of those days was little more than a large family circle, but when Linda Brauckmann — then Linda Scharfe — learned to skate in Vancouver under the eye of veteran coach Otto Gold, one of her fellow students was a young visitor from Chicago named Slavka Kohout. In later years the two would meet again many times, in different parts of the world; Linda as coach of Karen Magnussen; Slavka as coach of Janet Lynn, Karen's longtime rival.)

Linda Brauckmann's great love is music. Her

mother was a concert violinist; her step-father, a prominent gynecologist, was also a talented musician who had once turned down offers to play saxophone with the Guy Lombardo orchestra. The family home was filled with music; the two grand pianos and four saxophones were taken for granted. Linda herself became an excellent pianist.

"With me, music is a personal thing. I choose the music for all my skating programs before working on the choreography. And I have to go with the music I like. I have to be the one to do it. I can't listen to other people's opinions. Always you have to have in the back of your mind what will suit the skater's personality and ability.

"I spend hours and hours listening to music, and browsing through dusty old music shelves. Sometimes I get panicky when I can't find what I'm looking for . . . but usually I start far enough ahead to plan it out.

"One of the selections we put together for Karen a few years ago was a Gershwin thing. I thought it was great, but it wasn't quite Karen's bag. It had too many ups and downs in it, where she likes to just start and keep going. Her programs have never had much of a slow part in them.

"This year (1973) people told me Rachmaninoff, with piano and orchestra, would never go over. But I thought to myself, 'you just watch.' "

But even with a natural talent like Karen's to work with, coaching is never easy, and Linda had her share of anxious moments. Especially with school figures, and particularly the small intricate loops.

"Loops are so nerve-wracking. They're hard enough for the skaters, and I could never stand to watch them. Kids can make such awful errors."

Karen confirms her coach's hang-up. "When they were announcing my marks for the loop, Mrs. Brauckmann used to go to the bathroom and flush the toilet, so she couldn't hear them!"

But Karen's school figures were not a weak part of her skating talent, despite the overshadowing acclaim for her free-skating performances. "In her younger years, she always won on her free-skating," says Linda. "But I always thought her potential was just as great in figures, if we could just get it all together . . . and this, of course, is the way it turned out.

"I figured she was the best in the world long before she won the title, because she could do both. That's why she won all three gold medals at Bratislava."

But it was still the exciting free-skating routines that caught the imagination of crowds wherever Karen skated.

"There are few skaters in the world who can do split jumps both ways and flying camels with such beautiful positions as she has," says Linda. "But it took years to develop these things. I remember we worked on that camel for eighteen months before putting it in the program. We worked every day on the barrier, getting the position.

1/ She was six years old and the second-hand skates cost five dollars, when Karen first started skating at Vancouver's Kerrisdale Arena. But 15 years later this little girl was to become champion of the world.

2/ The first of hundreds! Karen won her first trophy at the age of seven / in a one and one-half minute free-skating competition at the Kerrisdale Club. The trophy is still competed for / now more eagerly than ever.

3/ A coach and his two starlets. Dr. Hellmut May with Karen (left) and her long-time friend and rival, Cathy Lee Irwin, who was to become runner-up in the Canadian championships 13 years later. Picture was taken in 1960.

4/ "The Snowflake Who Became a World Champion" ran the newspaper stories after the 1973 world champion victory. And this is the snowflake ballerina— Karen at the age of 10— rehearsing for a club carnival.

5/ The Magnussen Spiral— not famous when this picture was taken in 1964 (when 11-year-old Karen became the Canadian junior champion), but soon to become a classic in the world of figure skating.

6/ *Karen, age 13, strikes pose outside North Vancouver's North Shore Winter Club during the winter of 1966.*

CANADIAN PRESS PHOTO

7/ *Fine example of a mazurka, performed by Karen in practice at the North Shore Winter Club in 1968.*

KIYO OF HOLIDAY STUDIO

8/ Champion of Canada for the first time! Karen hugs trophy and bouquet after capturing the first of her five senior ladies' titles, at Vancouver in 1968.

TIM HUNTINGDON

9/ Karen at age 15 in Leningrad during 1968 I.S.U. tour, performing "Second-hand Rose" show number.

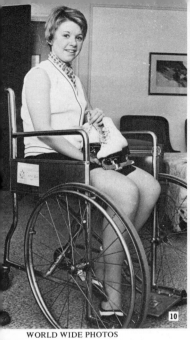

10/ Stress fractures of both legs, discovered on eve of 1969 world championships, forced Karen into a wheelchair. She covered the event for a Vancouver newspaper, then turned her check over to Bursary Fund for young skaters.

11/ Smiles on the faces of Karen and coach Linda Brauckmann tell the story. This was Karen's first time back on skates, just 36 days after she suffered fractures of both legs in Colorado Springs.

12/ Karen and an old friend, former Canadian men's champion Jay Humphry, also of North Vancouver, exchange anecdotes off the ice in 1969.

13/ Karen is amused by one of the 'welcome home' speeches after winning her first international medal— a bronze for third place— in world championships at Lyon, France, 1971.

KIYO OF HOLIDAY STUDIO

COY POE, PHOTO, SUN VALLEY

GORD CROUCHER, VANCOUVER PROVINCE

14/ *Karen is followed off the plane by her mother, Mrs. Gloria Magnussen, on returning home after winning her first international medal.*

15/ *Soaring through the air, Karen takes off on a beautiful scissor split, part of a unique combination in which she does two such splits, first with the right leg forward, then with the left.*

16/ *Rink at Sun Valley, Idaho, provides ideal setting for a perfect demonstration of an inside spread eagle—a graceful move, requiring considerable muscle control and skill.*

17/ *"Just one more picture, please, Karen" is a phrase she has heard a million times. This picture was taken at Vancouver's new Van Dusen Botanical Gardens.*

18/ Unusual occurrence in Vancouver! Cold snap produced frozen outdoor ponds, and Karen took advantage to practice. The North Shore mountains provide the picturesque backdrop.

GORD CROUCHER, VANCOUVER PROVINCE

19/ Ballet instruction has always formed part of Karen's total approach to figure skating. This photo was taken at North Shore Winter Club with dance instructor Norman Leggett.

*20/ Mutual admirers with much in common—
Karen and Barbara Ann Scott. Now Mrs. King,
Barbara Ann was Canada's first-ever world
skating champion (in 1947 and 1948).*
HARRISON, TORONTO SUN

21/ *"Raindrops Keep Falling on my Head" was the song which Karen helped make eve more famous, through her unique show routine, which sh performed while holding a sm umbrella in one hand.*

22/ *University exams still had to be passed, despite the gruelling training schedule Karen set for herself in 1972. Here she takes a few moments to study, between sessions on the North Shore Winter Club ice.*

23/ *Just a simple pose—taken during the Canadian championships held in Londor Ontario, in 1972.*

23

GORD CROUCHER, VANCOUVER PROVINCE

24/ A great favorite with newspaper, radio and television people all over the world, Karen takes time out from a 1972 training session for a chat with newspaperman–author, Jeff Cross.

She was very strong in the back, so she had a better chance. But it's not just a matter of saying, 'Oh, we'll put this in this year,' and then going out and doing it. It takes a long time to perfect these things."

But the hours and weeks spent together, on "patch," on stroking, and all the skating basics, became apparent in Karen's improving technique, and in the growing rapport between coach and pupil. "She's been a friend, a mother and a coach all in one," says Karen. "Any time I wanted to talk about anything, she'd say 'Come on up.' This is very important. She knows me like a book. I just have to be looking a certain way, and she knows whether it's going to be a good day or not. It's so unusual, and so wonderful. She's exactly the person I've needed."

Linda Brauckmann has never competed with her pupil for the spotlight. Always, when press, radio, and television began to seek out this exciting new skating star, Linda moved quietly into the background.

"She hides from cameras and interviews," says Karen. "She's always let it be mine."

6

MOVING INTO THE MAJOR LEAGUES

*It was then that Canadian figure skating
officials became excited about her, and
instructed coach Linda Brauckmann to make
sure Karen got through the tests necessary
to qualify for international competition.*

Jim Proudfoot, *Toronto Star,* February, 1966

In 1965, Karen was thirteen, the junior champion of Canada – and at the crossroads.

This was the time for decisions. And after
weighing the odds, listening to the outpourings
of praise for their eldest daughter, the Magnussen family decided to be positive.

The junior championship victory at Calgary
moved Karen into senior competition at national
level for the first time. Now she was in the "major
leagues" of figure skating, up against some of
the best women skaters in the world. At the 1966
Canadian championships in Peterborough, Ontario, people came just to watch the new free-
skating whiz from the West. A crowd of close
to five thousand jammed Peterborough's Memo-
rial Arena for the ladies' final, many of them
undoubtedly there to watch Toronto's Petra
Burka, the current world title holder, defend her

Canadian crown, but many there also to watch Karen, the youngest competitor in the event.

It was the kind of challenge she could not resist. Karen placed fifth in the compulsory figures, in itself a fine performance in her first senior national competition. But the best was yet to come.

Her free-skating performance at Peterborough is still regarded by many as the most electrifying ever seen in the Canadian championships. It earned an ovation from the crowd. Dr. Suzanne Francis, an international judge, awarded her a mark of 5.9 (out of 6.0) for artistic impression – the highest mark in the competition, and higher by one-tenth of a point than the same judge's mark for the world champion Miss Burka.

When the marks were added up, Karen was in second-place in the free-skating section, right behind world champion Petra. Karen's program of double jumps, spins, spirals, and other difficult maneuvers was a new one for the occasion. She had been practicing it for only two months.

"Until today I didn't even like it," said Gloria Magnussen, as she watched her daughter's marks go up on the board. "But a 5.9 from a world judge like Suzie Francis is fantastic. I must go and give Karen another hug."

Karen finished in fourth place overall, but veteran observers there had seen enough to convince them that they had been watching a future champion.

"It was one of those unforgettable moments that make up for a lot of the tawdriness in sport. . . . The name is Karen Magnussen and that's one you can file away for future reference, because if ever a child had the aura of potential greatness about her, this is the girl," wrote Jim Proudfoot of the *Toronto Star*.

"There's no doubt that yesterday's showing established Karen as perhaps the finest young skating prospect developed in Canada since Petra herself emerged from junior competition. She's the heiress-apparent to Petra's Canadian, North American and World crowns. . . ." he wrote. "When all is said and done, 1966 may well be remembered as the year the skating world became aware there was a Karen Magnussen."

Doug Kimpel, manager of the Canadian team for the subsequent world championships in Davos, Switzerland, said, "This kid will be a world beater. I wish I could take her to Davos." Of course he couldn't. Only three girls could make the team. But there was always next year.

In 1967 Karen had to prepare herself as never before. The Canadian championships were scheduled for Toronto, and everyone was expecting another sizzling performance from the youngster who had captured their imagination the previous year. A good performance in Toronto could lead to a berth on the Canadian team for the North American championships in Montreal. And the world championships in Vienna. And the 1968 Olympic Games were only just around the corner.

In Toronto Karen finished second to Toronto's Valerie Jones. That meant she was going to skate for Canada, both at home and overseas.

In Montreal she placed fourth in the North American contest – an event won by Peggy Fleming, the American girl who had displaced Petra Burka as world champion. And at the world championships in Vienna, in her international debut, Karen repeated the scintillating free-skating of Peterborough, placing seventh in that portion of the championships and twelfth overall. It seemed there was no stopping the head-long rush to the top.

In 1968 the Canadian championships were held in Vancouver for the first time in eighteen years, a perfect time and setting for the next big breakthrough. Back at Kerrisdale Arena, where she had first learned to skate, Karen put on display everything she had learned in the nine years that had passed since those toddling days. In the six compulsory figures, she rocketed into first place, picking up a total of 1020.3 points. That was 22.3 points better than her nearest rival, former clubmate Lindsay Cowan.

Close to four thousand people jammed themselves into the old Kerrisdale rink for the free-skating finale. In the long history of the Canadian championships British Columbia had never won a senior ladies' crown. But here was young Karen Magnussen with the title literally in her grasp. And Karen didn't disappoint them. Wave after wave of applause followed her around the ice as she went through her exciting, demanding routine. The final, fast spin produced a sustained roar and a standing ovation from the overflow crowd.

The performance was more than enough for her to hang onto the lead she had picked up in the figures. Karen had literally raced away from the rest of the field. Her total accumulation was 1823.3 points, with the first-place vote of all seven judges. Linda Carbonetto of Toronto was second with 1718.7, 114.6 points behind. Miss Cowan, who suffered a fall and a sprained wrist, finished third with 1702.2 points.

"Yes, I guess I've never skated better than that," said Karen afterwards. "It felt very good."

For the enthusiastic Vancouver fans, it felt very good indeed. In addition to Karen's massive triumph, B.C. captured all four senior titles for another West Coast 'first' – Jay Humphry won the men's championship, the pairs went to the brother-and-sister team of Betty and John Mc-Killigan, and the ice-dancing crown to Joni Graham and Don Phillips. And watching quietly in the background, as his daughter was mobbed by fans, was Alf Magnussen, smiling at questions about tension.

"You just stand back and hope that everything will be all right," he said. "But there is nothing you can do – she is all by herself out there. All you can do is stand on the side, feel very fortunate, and perspire very freely."

For the next few weeks, Alf perspired a little

more. The Winter Olympics were scheduled for Grenoble, France, with the world championships right afterwards in Geneva, Switzerland. No time for Karen to fly back home in between.

Grenoble and Geneva were the swan-song of Peggy Fleming. The dark-haired, graceful U.S. champion took a handsome lead in the compulsory figures of the Olympics, then put on a free-skating performance that produced a mark of 5.9 (out of the maximum 6.0) from every one of the nine judges for her "artistic impression." Seldom have international judges shown such unanimity. East Germany's Gaby Seyfert finished second, while the bronze medal went to Hana Maskova of Czechoslovakia.

Karen? The little Canadian champion placed eighth in judges' placements, tenth in total points, after the figures section. Not bad at all, considering that most competitors were three or four years older.

But it was the free-skating that made the Grenoble spectators sit up and stare. Writing in *The Times* of London, skating expert Dennis Bird commented: "The revelation of the evening was the excellence of the Canadian girls. The 15 year-old Karen Magnussen is a skater of great potential, whose athletic jumps and well-centred spins gave her fourth place in the free-skating. . . ."

Former U.S. champion Monty Hoyt, covering the Games for the esteemed *Christian Science Monitor,* wrote: "All eyes were riveted on the defending champions, but a young Canadian skater eclipsed their performances with an electrifying program that put her name on every tongue. . . ." Overall, Karen finished seventh, but almost without exception her name went into Olympic notebooks as the girl to watch in the next Games, four years distant.

Among those making the long-range prediction was Peggy Fleming's coach, Carlo Fassi: "Without a doubt, Karen Magnussen impressed me the most. She skated very, very well – with lots of life. She's the girl who could win – who *should* win – in 1972."

In Geneva, the world championships followed the same pattern. Now everyone was watching Karen. And, as in almost every case, the Olympic and world events produced almost identical results. Karen was seventh out of a field of thirty-two at Grenoble, seventh of twenty-two at Geneva.

The invitations for skating appearances poured in from all over the world, everyone wanting to take a look at the young girl who had even the most case-hardened professionals ecstatic.

There was the phone call that arrived one Monday morning as the Magnussen family was at breakfast. "This is Berlin," said the voice. "Berlin, Germany. Listen, Karen, the Berlin Skating Club is celebrating its 75th anniversary on Sunday, Monday, and Tuesday next week . . . we've got this fantastic ice-show lined up and we want you to be a part of it . . . bring your skates."

Two quick telephone calls were made in return – one to Ottawa to get official permission, the other to Germany to check that the invitation was real. And within forty-eight hours, Karen was zooming off to Berlin.

7

WHEN THE BLACK CLOUDS FORMED

Remember that newspaper headline after I hit the boards and put my teeth through my lip? . . . "Smash, bash, crash. . . . Karen Prevails Over All." What a way to make the papers!

It was, in every way, a very bad year.

At the 1969 Canadian championships in Toronto, Karen lost her senior title to a little blond whirlwind named Linda Carbonetto. It was a close contest, four of the seven judges voting for Linda, the other three for Karen. But many in Maple Leaf Gardens on the night of the final felt that something was wrong, somehow, somewhere.

Karen had led in figures, but her free-skating performance was not up to par. She seemed strained. Her smile was forced rather than relaxed and confident.

Miss Carbonetto put on the free-skating display of her young life before the hometown fans, and became the new Canadian champion. It was a bitter blow, but . . . "I learned a lot from that," reflects Karen. "It sure made me come back fighting hard. But I just wasn't myself in that competition. It was the only year I can remember that I couldn't get myself up for a championship. I am usually so excited and ready to go, but in Toronto my heart just wasn't in it."

Then came Oakland, California, and more trouble.

The North American championships, a competition between Canada and the United States, were held every two years, alternating between sites in the two countries. In 1969 Oakland was the location, which meant four U.S. judges to three Canadians, in the adopted system of adjudication.

"I was feeling a lot better in California than I had in Toronto," says Karen. "I was skating well, and I felt great when I won the compulsory figures section over Linda Carbonetto and all the American girls.

"I skated my heart out in the free-skating, landed all my jumps and really did 100 per cent better than in Toronto. So it came as a really crushing blow when they gave the championship to someone else." (Janet Lynn won by just 1.4 points, with Karen second.)

"It was shattering," says Karen, "but I learned a lot from it. It was an eye-opener, my first experience of the politics involved in skating.

"The next night the ice-dancing championship was given to a Canadian couple over the Americans, to try to make up for the mistake made the previous evening – which only proved what a big mistake it was! Because [U.S. champions]

Jim Sladky and Judy Schwomeyer were so superior to Bruce Lennie and Donna Taylor [the Canadian dance couple]. They're wonderful kids, Bruce and Donna, but they were ranked twelfth or so in the world, while Sladky and Schwomeyer were third or fourth.

"The whole thing was crazy. If that hadn't been done in the dance competition, people would just have said 'Well, I guess they had their reasons for what happened in the ladies' event,' but there was no justification for them to pull that on their own kids.

"Right then I thought, 'Wow! Why am I worrying about this? If they'll do that to their own American kids, they're certainly going to do it to someone else.'"

There were few observers of the Oakland scene who did not agree, at least in part, with those sentiments. British critic Sandra Stevenson wrote later in *The Guardian:* ". . . the outcry was so great that the judges felt obliged to rectify the decision by giving the dance event to the Canadians at a time when Sladky and Schwomeyer were ranked third in the world. . . ."

Sports editor Jim Proudfoot of the *Toronto Star* wrote: "The judging was so laughably inconsistent that Canadian officials admitted they'd begun to question the value of participation in any form."

Columnist Denny Boyd wrote in the *Vancouver Sun:* "The same crooks who stole the ladies' championship from Karen Magnussen made up for their crime by giving Canada the dance championship they stole from two Americans. I am making a recommendation to the editor that the next time the U.S. and Canada meet in figure-skating competition we send our police reporter."

(The North American championships were to pass away, unlamented, in 1972, but not before Karen had had a chance to reverse the decision over Miss Lynn in the 1971 event, the last North Americans to be held. Even two of the three U.S. judges voted her into first place on that occasion!)

However, the bad taste of Oakland carried over into the world championships that followed two weeks later in Colorado Springs. East Germany's Gaby Seyfert, a strong, stylish skater, was favored to win the ladies' crown relinquished by Peggy Fleming of the U.S. But the battle between Karen Magnussen and Janet Lynn, a few notches down the list, was a hot topic of discussion.

Between the two championships, Karen went to Squaw Valley, California, to polish her program for the world event. "I'd been feeling some pain in my legs for quite a while," she recalls. "It actually started in early October, but I thought I was just out of condition from the summer and that if I really worked, my muscles would get stronger and there'd be no more problem. The pain would come and go, and I would take an afternoon off now and then to ease it. Brian Power, who conducted exercise classes at our club, said he thought it might be a case of shin splints, but I thought if I just kept on going the pain would disappear.

"It wasn't too bad at the Canadians in Toronto and I had hardly any pain at all at North Americans, but one morning at Squaw Valley the pain came back and started working into the backs of my legs. It got so bad I had to get off the ice right away. "I went to see a doctor and his diagnosis was 'pulled Achilles tendons.' So it was back on the ice, then over to Colorado Springs for the final practices.

"On the Sunday evening we were practicing when I felt a pain like a sledgehammer was hitting me in both legs. Both my feet were beginning to swell. However, Tenley Albright [former world champion and now a doctor] was there and said, 'I'm sure you'll be fine in the competition tomorrow. You're skating so well!' But the pain was so bad I had to be taken to hospital in Colorado Springs to see a bone specialist. He gave me a sequence of tests, some of which I just couldn't do at all, like rolling up my toes, and took some X-rays.

"It was midnight by this time, with the championships starting the next day, when the specialist came back with the verdict: 'No way you can skate, my dear. You have stress fractures in both legs.' I couldn't believe it. I thought 'You're kidding!' And then I said to myself, 'They can't stop me skating. I'm going to skate!' But the doctor gave it to me straight, and really scared me. He said that if I went on, I might never skate again.

"That was it. I had to listen to the doctor, finally. I was to stay in a wheelchair. Tenley Albright came up again the next day while I was sitting by the side of the rink and said, 'My God, if you can skate like that with two broken legs, what are you going to do next year?' "

But, right there in Colorado Springs, next year seemed a long time away. The wheelchair was to be official transportation for a while, and beyond that lay only uncertainty.

Injury was no stranger to Karen. Like many skaters, she knew all about the bumps and bruises that accompany the strenuous activity of ice-skating. One of her legs had been broken before; when she was six, a slab of marble fell on it. In the B.C. Coast championships in 1964 at the North Shore Winter Club, she tripped over something on the ice and crashed headlong into the boards, putting her teeth through her lip. That was during the warmup session, but after taking time out for treatment Karen went back out again to win the senior ladies' championship! The following year, in a warmup for an exhibition appearance in Kamloops, British Columbia, she took another spill, crashing headlong into the boards and being rushed to hospital with concussion. Again she came back the following night, even though it was only a brief appearance.

"I usually manage to find the only hole in the ice," she told anxious enquirers.

And at the 1968 Winter Olympics in Grenoble, France, she put a skate blade right through the other boot and into her foot while attempting a jump. Yet Karen still managed to finish in seventh place among the world's top skaters, five places better than in the world championships the previous year.

So by the end of 1969, Karen could look back over a period marked by both triumph and tribulation. It was a time during which her courage and determination had been put to severe tests.

It remained to be seen whether that courage could steel her for the challenges which still lay ahead.

8

THE TOUGHEST KIND OF TEST

I never once thought about quitting. My only worry was that I might not be able to do as well after the injuries as I had done before.

There were some who would have written her off as a contender for world honors. But Karen herself never doubted her ability to overcome the setbacks that had temporarily halted her career. And there was comfort and encouragement in the hundreds of letters, cards, and telegrams that arrived from all parts of the world. Commitments for appearances in shows and carnivals had to be broken. But, "come anyway," replied many. And to a number of events – fund-raising dinners, receptions, speaking engagements – Karen trundled her wheelchair.

Though the doctors and specialists had predicted a three-month period of immobility, it was April 1, 1969 – three days before her seventeenth birthday and only thirty-six days after the fateful words of doctors in Colorado Springs – that she laced on her skates once again. Under the watchful eye of coach Linda Brauckmann, and with the guarded approval of her doctors, Karen stepped on to the ice at the North Shore Winter

Club, took a few hesitant steps, beamed, and said, "Gosh, that feels wonderful."

The hairlines indicating the fractures on the legs were rapidly disappearing and the doctors were now confident of a perfect recovery.

After reading the X-rays, the specialists gave her the okay to get back on the ice, and within a month Karen was able to take part in the annual carnival at the North Shore Winter Club. Later that summer, at Sun Valley, Idaho, she proved that her sights were once again set on the championship target.

The Sun Valley Skating Club's bulletin for that summer session said briefly: "Karen Magnussen, the 1968 Canadian champion, proved to be the hit of the final ice show and also provided her fans with the pleasure of watching her take the U.S. Figure Skating Association and International Skating Union dance tests."

Those legs were obviously in good enough shape for Karen to skate in shows. Good enough to pass national and international merit tests. Would they be strong enough to hold up under the constant pressure of practice for championship competition, and for the championships themselves?

The first real test came in January, at the 1970 Canadian championships in Edmonton, Alberta. Linda Carbonetto had turned professional. Advance publicity hinted that the battle for the ladies' crown would turn out to be a duel between Karen and her old friend and rival, Cathy

Lee Irwin, now skating out of Toronto. But, from the outset, there was no doubt about the result.

For the first of the six compulsory figures, Karen placed first with all seven judges. On the second figure she was first with six judges, and tied for first with the other one. At the completion of the compulsory section she was ahead of the field by 20.9 points. A North Shore clubmate, Mary McCaffrey, was second; Cathy Lee Irwin was fourth.

Then the free-skating – the jumps, the spirals, the spins – would the legs stand the strain? Her first moments on the ice were agonizing for those who watched. In the seven-minute warmup session before her performance, Karen twice attempted that old tester, the double axel. Both times she missed the jump.

Face serious and drawn, she went around and tried it again. Still it wasn't right. Then she drew the attention of officials to something on the ice, a bobbypin dropped by a previous competitor. It had to be scraped out. Such things have been known to cause serious injury when caught in a blade.

Finally it came Karen's turn to skate – by the luck of the draw, last of the fifteen entrants. Still frowning with concentration, she took off on her four-minute routine. Two split jumps, faultlessly performed, and the frown began to disappear. Then the double axel. No problem. A fine landing, and the first trace of a smile. Into a flying sit-spin, cheers from the audience, and now a delighted grin. Stronger and stronger to a whirlwind finish. Deafening applause from the packed Edmonton Gardens audience. They had seen enough to convince them that Karen was once again their champion.

So had the judges. All seven first-place votes plumped solidly for the girl who had fought her way back to the top. And when the Canadian selection committee announced the lineup of the national team for the upcoming 1970 world championships in Ljubljana, Yugoslavia, there was the name of Karen Magnussen at the head of the list.

9

THE LONG, LONELY HOURS

I never left school, and I'd advise other young skaters to do the same. It's important, because you need friends outside of skating. And the discipline of keeping up with school, classes, and lessons, reinforces the disciplines involved in learning spins and spirals.

Sonja Henie started it all. When the dimpled Norwegian blond won the first of her ten world championships in 1927, figure skating was not much more than a pleasant pastime. Who remembers, for instance, that the previous holder of the world title was one Herma Jaross-Szabo of Austria?

By the time Miss Henie left Norway for Hollywood in 1936, things had changed. Figure skating had become an established international sport, but was still more glamorous than athletic. The arrival of the North Americans on the scene had much to do with changing that concept. (The first Canadians had competed in the world championships in 1928, but Canada did not win a world title until Barbara Ann Scott's 1947 victory at Stockholm.)

As double and then triple jumps were added

to the repertoire of the most accomplished skaters, physical conditioning became a major factor in national and international competition. Skaters like Dick Button, Donald Jackson, and the Jenkins brothers, Hayes and David, moved figure-skating off the entertainment pages to newspaper sports sections. Later, longtime observers of the amazing change would swear that, were Sonja Henie still competing, she would find it hard to win even a novice competition.

Girl skaters were slower to adapt to the more athletic concept. Few were able to attain the new high standards of physical strength and ability, without sacrificing feminity or the sophistication and glamor of the sport. Karen Magnussen was one of the few.

After her traumatic experience with fractured legs on the eve of the 1969 world championships, Karen had made an inspired comeback to recapture the Canadian title in 1970. It was then that she needed total dedication if she were ever to make it to the top.

Long, lonely hours tracing figures on the ice, dawn-after-dawn workouts to keep muscles supple and strong – these were the main considerations. But school books could never be shelved, and there were still home chores to be shared. It was the same pattern as before, but now it was intensified.

She had graduated from Carson Graham High School and enrolled as a first-year student at the newly established Simon Fraser University, where sport and athletics hold a prominent place in the curriculum. Now her days were filled with all-out effort, a round of non-stop activity that would stun most professional athletes.

A typical week on the Magnussen calendar went like this:

Sunday: Skating practice with coach Linda Brauckmann from 7 a.m. to 10:30 a.m. Back home for studies (English, history, political science, and kinesiology). Then a brisk run up and down the North Shore hills near her home until 5 p.m. Help with the evening meal – especially if there was baking to be done – followed by more studying. And bed by 8 p.m.

Monday: Up at 5 a.m. for a hearty breakfast. On the ice at the North Shore Winter Club for practice by 6:15. A three-hour session of skating before reporting for classes at the university at 9:30 a.m. Classes until 3 p.m., then back on the ice until 6 o'clock. Home to prepare dinner. More studying. And bed.

Wednesdays and Thursdays followed the Monday pattern. On Tuesdays and Fridays there were no university classes, which meant more time for skating, from 7 a.m. to 3:30 p.m. Tuesday evening was devoted to ballet class and Friday evening to ballet and modern jazz lessons.

The thirty-five hours of skating each week would be more than enough for any but the most disciplined athlete. Yet there was more. Every two weeks came a session with a chiropractor, for manipulation to ease the strain on back muscles caused by the pounding sustained in the soaring jumps.

And she was also a guinea pig. As part of her training program, Karen had volunteered, along with other athletes, to take part in kinesiology studies with Dr. Stan Brown at the University of British Columbia. They produced some interesting reports.

"The tests showed that figure skating ranked high in terms of physical requirements," says Karen. "For instance, one statistic showed that four minutes of hard skating equaled one hour of basketball."

At SFU, Karen volunteered for more of the same. Four times a week under the careful scrutiny of Dr. Eric Bannister, head of the kinesiology department, other medical observers, and SFU football coach Tom Walker, the Canadian champion submitted herself to the ultimate in athletic exertion. Coach Walker explained the routine: "The exercises measured the maximum capacity of Karen's oxygen transport system. On the ergometer [a sort of training bicycle] and the treadmill, she pushed herself to the point of maximum exertion, while all the results were carefully measured and recorded."

How did Karen measure up? "She's not just average, she's super," said Walker. "In technical terms, her body has the maximum capacity to use 47.6 milliliters of oxygen per kilogram of body weight per minute. The average girl college student would register about thirty-five on this scale. And, although this has not formed part of the scientific study, we're all tremendously impressed with her absolute mental toughness and ability to drive herself to the maximum."

Toughness? Physical exertion? Wasn't it all very unfeminine? A picture was the best answer. Photographer Dave Paterson, on assignment from the *Vancouver Daily Province*, was dispatched to take a series of pictures of the Magnussen training schedule, particularly the "push to the ultimate" tests at the university. One of his shots made almost every daily paper in Canada, many in the U.S.A., and the wirephoto networks of Canadian Press and Associated Press.

It showed Karen, in halter top and shorts, astride the ergometer, with wires and gauges attached to all parts of her anatomy. This girl not feminine? Dozens of photo-editors didn't buy that.

Some conservative readers tut-tutted. But Karen's reaction was typically feminine. "I wonder if they sent it to Playboy?" she said with an impish giggle.

Ballet classes helped her retain her femininity despite the daily physical grind. And here again she was lucky.

During the Russian revolution of 1917, one of the talented artists forced to flee the country had been Madame Lydia Karpova, a friend of the great Anna Pavlova, and a fellow student with the legendary Nijinsky, Balanchine, and Fokine at the St. Petersburg Imperial School. Karpova, still ranked as one of the world's greatest ballet teachers, eventually found her way to Vancouver. And it was in her strict, formal rehearsal rooms that Karen added the qualities of classical ballet to her other considerable talents.

"At that time I was actually doing more dancing than skating – five times a week – with Madame," says Karen. "She followed the old tradition of Russian ballet schools. We all had to curtsy to her when we came in, and applaud her when the lesson was finished. She was an absolutely fascinating person. At the age of seventy-three she was still agile enough to lead us through a Spanish dancing session."

Thus, in an all-consuming atmosphere of classical ballet, modern jazz, the maximum in fitness training, and thirty-five hours of skating each week, Karen prepared herself mentally and physically for the assault on the pinnacle.

10

MAGNUSSEN AGAINST THE WORLD!

In the magic of the moment, Nancy Greene was asked if, as a fellow British Columbian and as Canada's only medal winner at the previous Winter Olympics, she would stop by the press room and share a sentiment or two with the new heroine of Canadian Olympiana.

Entitled to do so as a member of the working press – by virtue of her CBC television duties – Nancy bowed out decisively.

"Heck, no," she said. "This is Karen's day."

From the moment of Karen's smashing Canadian championship victory in 1970, there was little doubt that she represented her country's main hope for international honors.

In international skating there can be no standing still or marking time. You press steadily upwards or you drop back. And once a skater starts to slide in competition, that is the beginning of the end. So many other talented skaters are pressing from behind, trying to overtake, that any slip is fatal. Karen was climbing inexorably, rung by rung.

Prior to the 1967 calamity at Colorado

Springs, she had placed twelfth in her 1967 world debut and seventh in both the Olympics and world championships of 1968. Her rival, Janet Lynn of the United States, made her first world appearance in 1968 and placed ninth, jumping to fifth in 1969 while Karen watched from her wheelchair.

That could easily have been the overtaking point. But, at the world championships of 1970 in Ljubljana, Karen put on a dazzling display to finish fourth, while Janet dropped a notch to sixth place. The old order had been restored.

At the 1971 championships in Lyon, France, Karen won her first international medal, a bronze for third place behind Austria's stalwart Trixi Schuba and stylish Julie Holmes of the United States. Janet finished fourth, but in the presentation ceremonies after the event, someone managed to find a separate podium for her. And, while the three medal winners were at center ice to receive their awards, the A.B.C. cameras trained on Janet, as a commentator explained that, while Miss Lynn had not finished in the first three, she had captured the hearts of the French audience and the cheers were all for her. Miss Schuba, clear winner on the strength of her extraordinarily skillful school figures, had to be consoled on the podium by the other medal winners, Julie and Karen.

There were others who were upset by the incident, among them U.S. team manager Charles DeMore, who later apologized to the Magnussens. And back in the hotel that evening, where the medalists were holding separate victory parties, Karen marched across the hall to the Austrian reception, grabbed Trixi by the hand, and ushered her into the Canadian rooms with the phrase, "Now I'd like you all to applaud the real world champion!"

That was 1971, and it was more than ever obvious that a Magnussen-Lynn confrontation was just around the corner.

The following year brought the Olympics. The Winter Games were set for Sapporo, Japan, to be followed, three weeks later, by the world championships in Calgary, Alberta. On Karen's shoulders rested almost all of Canada's hopes for an Olympic medal.

"It's Magnussen against the world," cried one newspaper headline. And so it proved.

Karen and her two old friends from Kerrisdale juvenile days, Ruth Hutchinson and Cathy Lee Irwin, comprised the ladies' skating team for the Games. Unfortunate Ruth, the victim of many freak accidents and injuries in her career, broke an arm at the Olympic Village on the way back from a practice session, and had to withdraw. Cathy skated a fine program but could manage no better than thirteenth place. Among the top girls, Trixi Schuba had taken her usual big lead in figures and was able to sit back and watch the others try to catch her.

Julie Holmes tried, but her rather flat program found little favor with the judges. Janet also tried, but a fall from a flying sit-spin marred her performance. Janet did move ahead of Julie into temporary hold of second place, however. It was now solely up to Karen.

Facing an impossible gap of 141.3 points behind the front-running Austrian girl, Karen made a magnificent attempt. She slashed Trixi's margin in half. It was not enough to win, but more than enough to capture the silver medal, Canada's only medal from the Sapporo Games, and to serve notice that she was the principal challenger at the upcoming world championships.

In Calgary, with a packed Stampede Corral audience roaring approval, Karen inched even closer to the world title. Trailing Trixi by 130.5 points after the school figures, she poured it on in the free-skating finale to earn a standing ovation. The final margin was a mere 33.3 points. More important in the overall tally, Karen had picked up the first-place votes of three of the nine judges, including the American, while Trixi had the other six.

It was a fitting climax to thrilling years of competition, years of all-out effort and almost non-stop travel. Globe-trotting had introduced a whole new life style to the girl from North Vancouver. In Tokyo she and Sammy Davis Jr. exchanged Easter baskets. In Moscow she visited the Imperial Dance School where Madame Karpova had trained with Pavlova. When she talked to Denmark's Princess (later Queen) Margarethe in Copenhagen, they discovered they had something in common – Swedish mothers. And back home in Vancouver, her status had earned her a place at the head table with visiting Queen Elizabeth and Prince Philip.

Celebrities, show business personalities, high-ranking government leaders – all were as pleased to meet her as she was to meet them. But not even this taste of the high life could turn the head of the determined young lady away from her goal, the world championship.

She had kicked adversity in the teeth, taken the political slurs with a smile, and now, at the age of twenty, she was ready for her final challenge. Bratislava was just around the bend.

11

EVERYONE UNDER THE SPELL

*Television is the big thing now. It's doing an
awful lot for figure skating, bringing it right out
in the open, where everyone can see it.*

The harassed television sports commentator was
an old friend. We had done some broadcasts together, years before. But when we met again, in
the small British Columbia town where he now
worked, his greeting was frantic.

"Look, I have to do an interview show with
Karen Magnussen tonight. And I don't know the
first thing about figure skating. What the hell do
I ask her?"

I laughed, because the same kind of situation
had arisen many times before. Karen Magnussen,
the biggest attraction in Canadian figure skating,
was in town. She was willing to do an interview,
to answer questions. But where to find someone
who knew the right kind of question to ask?

I gave him a couple. First, ask her for an
opinion on the claim that figure skating is a
"sissy" sport, then sit back and listen. If you need
another lead later on, ask her to run the rule
over the other kids who are competing here.

That should take care of your half-hour show comfortably. She'll look after it.

He stared at me. Two questions? To a young girl who will say "yes" or "no" and giggle all the time? You must be crazy. Still unconvinced, he jotted down the questions and went away, shaking his head.

I missed his TV show, but the next day he bounced up to me in the arena where the B.C. championships were being held. "I didn't believe it, but you were absolutely right," he said. "She was just bloody marvelous. It was one of the best interviews I've ever done."

Many admiring tributes and millions of words of praise have been lavished on Karen Magnussen in her career. So much so that skeptics dismiss them as pure propaganda, churned out by some monster machine. Yet in the newspaper and magazine editorial rooms, radio and television booths, the people responsible for the material readily confess to being Magnussen boosters.

"She doesn't just turn the personality on and off – it's real."

"How can you not be impressed . . . she has it all."

"I honestly tried to find a flaw in that charm, so help me. But now I'm her biggest fan."

There's no big secret to the charisma that has often been referred to as "the Magnussen magic." Karen just likes people. Some of her classes in her first year at Simon Fraser University were geared to a possible future in public relations.

"I think that's what I might like to do . . . sometime in the future," she says. "I enjoy meeting people. And, outside of skating, I can't think of anything that would be more interesting."

Particularly in Canada, but also in many other parts of the world, she has given figure skating a bright, healthy image – a young lady from Vancouver who is a superb athlete, an artist, and a delightful personality all in one.

I remember sharing a beer in the Bratislava press room with Franz Joseph Darius, a huge, blond, bearded West German free-lance writer whose forte is covering auto racing, but who inclines to figure skating as a pleasant sideline.

"Dammit, if that girl doesn't win, it'll be the crime of the century," he growled, when it looked as if Karen's bid for the title might come up short.

Many other writers and broadcasters have fallen equally under the spell of the big blue eyes and the classic temperament. And some are worth remembering.

Ray Wilson, a former champion skater, writing in the British *Ski and Skate* magazine about the 1970 world championships in Ljubljana, had this to say: "Then came a program which to me was the finest performance I have seen by a lady skater. Karen Magnussen of Canada was the skater, the girl who watched last year's championships in Colorado Springs with two broken legs. And yet here she was, just over a year later, skating so beautifully – superlatives escape me. The interpretation of the beautiful music, the difficulty, the originality – all were first class. Karen, you were marvellous, and I remain, sincerely, your number one fan."

Dennis Bird, the astute skating critic of *The Times* of London, watched the same performance and had this to say in an article for Britain's *Skating World:* "Finally there were two of the finest performances I have ever seen in women's free skating. One was given by a girl who, last year, broke both her legs – Karen Magnussen of Canada. [The other performance referred to was by East Germany's Gaby Seyfert, the overall winner in 1970.] By an appropriate coincidence Karen was skating on the very day that Graham Hill, the former world champion racing motorist, made his vigorous comeback in the South African Grand Prix after a similar double fracture.

"What courage, determination and fortitude both these stars of world sport have shown in their fight back to the top. Karen skated brilliantly at Ljubljana, with a spontaneous gaiety that contrasted with the grim, dour or apprehensive countenances so many skaters adopt on these occasions. Her lovely, clean jumps showed she indeed recovered. She was third in free skating, has indeed recovered. She was third in free skating, fourth in final ranking – the best results yet for an attractive 18 year-old whose name will surely resound throughout the skating world for several years to come."

By the following year, the same writer had confirmed his opinion. From Lyon, France, Dennis Bird wrote: "The music of Rachmaninoff inspired a fine performance by Canadian and North American champion Karen Magnussen. To my mind, she is the supreme stylist in women's skating today."

In many towns where Karen has skated, I have seen the same thing happen. Flinty sports reporters, chagrined at having to cover "this figure skating thing" have fallen under the spell and become converts, at least for the duration of the championships.

Reyn Davis had this to say in the *Winnipeg Free Press* after the Canadian championships of 1971: "When Karen Magnussen skates you can almost hear her teeth grit through that smile. She is so determined, it is difficult to imagine anything standing in her way. With Karen it's a one-way street to success . . . there's nothing, absolutely nothing wrong with her determination. It's her trademark and Karen Magnussen intends to stamp the world with it."

Back in 1968, Michael Hanlon wrote in the *Canadian* magazine: "Early success doesn't appear to have made her conceited or even convinced her how good she is. She doesn't brag about her achievements, keeps cuttings and programs more as souvenirs than as a record of her conquests . . . . she knows, no matter how good she is, she has to be better if she is really going to be the tops."

As lavish as they have been with praise for their favorite girl, sportswriters generally have been equally quick with biting sarcasm when Karen found her progress blocked by other influences.

"Miss Magnussen was patently jobbed in the North American championships at Oakland, when four American judges contrived to give the title to little Janet Lynn of the U.S. The decision was so gamey that many people in the attendance expressed deep concern that there was a cargo of rotting fish unattended at the Oakland fish docks. One Canadian muttered: 'I know what those judges are doing. They're getting even with us for sending them Paul Anka.'" (Denny Boyd, in the *Vancouver Sun*.)

Like no other athlete in Canadian sport, Karen has produced a unanimity among newspaper columnists that is as surprising as it is articulate:

"B. J. Thomas sang Raindrops Keep Falling on My Head, but Butch Cassidy and the Sundance Kid and Karen Magnussen are making it famous . . . Cassidy and The Kid are a couple of fictitious characters in a million-dollar movie . . . but Karen is as real as Yum Yum Days in Manitoba." *(The Winnipeg Free Press.)*

"She gets standing ovations out of habit. She wears a smile as her passport into anyone's heart and carries captivating courage as a personal badge, no matter where she skates. She's spent a lot of the best years of any teenager's life carrying the fantastic dream of a country on her back – and if it's eaten away at her, she's told no one . . ." (Bob Hughes in the *Calgary Albertan.)*

Nowhere in the volumes of publicity Karen has received in the past fifteen years, can you find a paragraph, or a phrase, that would reject these statements. Clearly, if newspapermen had been the judges, Karen Magnussen would have been the champion of the world a long time before 1973.

12

THE POLITICS OF SKATING

In a way it's a shame that come next month we're going to have to share this jewel with the rest of the world. Karen is scheduled to take her Canadian crown to Bratislava at the end of February, and anybody who says she won't trade it in for the world title is begging for a punch in the mouth.

Clancy Loranger, *Vancouver Province,*
January, 1973

If there had been pressure before, it was mild compared to the Bratislava buildup. The pot had been kept simmering throughout the summer of '72 by what seemed endless television re-runs of previous championships, many of them geared – by accident or design – to stress the two-way battle for the ladies' championship between Karen and Janet Lynn. American televiewers, at least, might have been excused for believing that no one else of importance would be taking part in the 1973 championships.

As the championship season drew closer, the size and significance of the publicity buildup was increasingly evident. Canadian visitors to Europe, for example, brought back the message, "Everyone is talking about Janet Lynn . . . what's happened to Karen?"

What was happening was a mammoth propaganda buildup for the American girl. It was hard to define, but anyone connected with skating knew it existed. Examples prove nothing by themselves. But when they are added together and multiplied many times, they give some indication of what was happening backstage.

While the overture to Bratislava was being played, a well-read British sports magazine, with a file of handsome pictures of Karen on hand for eve-of-championship publication, instead appeared with a full-page color spread of Janet.

Again in England, Karen's name was significantly omitted from the list of skaters invited to take part in a special two-day gala at the Queen's Club in London, to be shown later on BBC television. The cost of flying the Canadian champion over was cited as the reason for the omission, but among those invited were East Germany's Christine Errath, Britain's Jean Scott, Dorothy Hamill of the United States and Janet Lynn — every other contender for the vacant world title.

A well-known British sports writer admitted privately to me that a top American skating official had told him there was no way Karen Magnussen could win the title "because the Canadian Figure Skating Association has neglected to do its homework in Europe . . ."

And, as mentioned earlier, the name of Karen

Magnussen just happened to be missing from the special championship brochure printed in several languages by the Czech organizing committee – a brochure that speculated on the possible outcome of the championships by suggesting Janet Lynn, Christine Errath, and Sonja Morgenstern as potential victors. Miss Lynn and Miss Morgenstern also rated pictures in the Czech brochure, but no mention of the Canadian challenger.

The most distressing of the events leading up to Bratislava was the television incident at the U.S. national championships that must be chronicled here again, as an example of the astonishing machinations preceding the world championships.

To do so, we must step back one small pace to January, a month before the world finals, and examine the national championships of Canada and the United States. The Canadian event was held in Vancouver from January 15 to 21. The U.S. championships came the following week, at Bloomington, Minnesota.

In Vancouver, Karen won the ladies' title for the fifth time, despite some less than enthusiastic judging, particularly in the school figures and the two-minute compulsory free-skating program. Men's champion Toller Cranston, an articulate, outspoken young man, was later to tell a press conference he regarded one judge's mark for Karen as "an insult." Canadian pairs champion Val Bezic was overheard to describe Karen's figures mark as "just ridiculous."

But, as always, the ladies' champion herself was philosophical. After completion of the third and final figure (double-three-change-double-three) she smiled ruefully. "It would be nice to think that I didn't have to keep proving myself. What do they want of me? I thought it was a good figure. I wouldn't say so otherwise. But then, they are the judges."

Karen's Canadian crown was never in jeopardy, however. Her formidable talent in all sections of the figure-skating art gave her the final first-place votes of all seven judges, though she was edged out marginally in the free-skating section by the exuberant, nothing-to-lose performance of Ottawa's sixteen-year-old Lynn Nightingale.

In the overall reckoning, Karen piled up 103.50 points with a perfect seven ordinals (all seven first-place votes). Her old friend and rival, Cathy Lee Irwin, was second with 96.80 points and 17 ordinals. And young Miss Nightingale was third with 83.60 points and 20 ordinals.

The following week in Bloomington, Janet Lynn found things a lot tougher in the bid to retain her U.S. championship. Janet fell behind in the figures (won by sixteen-year-old Diane Goldstein of Denver), then came to grief in the short compulsory program (a hint of things to come) won by another sixteen-year-old, Dorothy Hamill of Riverside, Connecticut.

Janet won the long free-skating program and managed to pick up the overall first-place votes of all seven judges, but her eventual margin of victory was less than two points (194.24 to 192.25) over second-place Miss Hamill.

The ABC-TV coverage of the U.S. championships showed the complete four-minute free-skating program of Miss Lynn, a fine effort to be sure, though neutral observers must have been surprised at the marks it received (three perfect 6.0's and the rest 5.9's).

Then the television program cut away from the U.S. championship action to show some film of the preceding week's event in Vancouver, obviously inviting viewers to compare the respective world title challenges of the two national champions. The Canadian film clip, lasting a few seconds, showed only the section in which Karen tripped over some dirt and tumbled to the ice. That was it! It was in the combination section of her program featuring a split-split-axel-double loop-butterfly-illusion, and the fall came on the axel takeoff.

"It's such an easy thing," says Karen. "I've never fallen on that in my life."

But her dirt-splattered boots adequately told the story of the fall. And this was the sequence the U.S. television audience saw. That was the extent of the U.S. coverage of the Canadian championships. Nothing more, nothing less, apart from some gratuitous remarks by commentator Dick Button suggesting that Janet Lynn's chances for the world title now appeared excellent, since the Canadian girl was obviously not skating well.

That was a low blow in sports journalism, and the amount of ill-feeling and contempt it generated was considerable and far-reaching. Columnist Jim Taylor, in the following day's editions of the *Vancouver Sun,* wrote:

"Ten minutes after the assassination attempt, Karen Magnussen received a telephone call from California. It was Peggy Fleming's mother, apologizing for the United States. Mrs. Fleming was upset because the same sort of shot had been fired at her daughter a few years earlier, from the same rifle, by the same marksman. 'She told me not to let it worry me', said Karen. 'Well, I don't plan to.'

"But while Karen might stay untouched by it all, other issues will be swirling around. The American propaganda machine – and to a lesser extent the Canadian – will be in full swing. 'When you get to Bratislava,' a figure skating lady told me, 'be sure to talk it up about Karen, how well she's skating, how good she is. They'll be doing it for Janet, really pouring it on, and you never know how much influence it can have on the judging.

"You'd hate to think it could be true. Yet many believe it, just as many believe the selected shot of Karen falling was not entirely accidental. 'Dick Button packages the show for ABC,' they say. 'He's pushing Janet. He always has. He'll be over there and that's all people will hear. Janet, Janet, Janet.' "

The anger of the public at the television show

was reflected by Karen, but in a different way. If it had been intended as a psychological move to depress the Canadian champion, it had the reverse effect. It produced a feminine ferocity that was formidable.

"If they'd wanted to pick one thing to make me more determined to skate and win, they couldn't have picked a better one," Karen said out loud.

But the pressure on both principal contenders for the world title was now tremendous, following these ill-conceived events. Karen had retained her Canadian crown comfortably enough, but was receiving virtually no acclaim outside her own country. Conversely, Janet had managed to retain her U.S. title by the narrowest of margins, yet was being hailed as the next world champion. It was an incongruous situation that not only ignored Karen's obvious claims to be the number one contender, but also completely overlooked the European girls who were about to compete for their own continental championship in Cologne, West Germany, notably the claim of East Germany's Christine Errath, who went on to win the European title.

Outside of her country, there appeared to be little support for the Canadian champion. One notable exception was *The Guardian*, the highly respected British newspaper whose skating writer, Sandra Stevenson, significantly had been the only correspondent to cover all three championships – Canadian, U.S., and European.

Said *The Guardian*, in its world championship

assessment: ". . . it might seem to millions that it is Miss Lynn's turn for the world title. But that would ignore Karen Magnussen, 20, of Canada, skating's Cinderella, who this season has been almost ignored by advance publicity, certainly in the U.S.A. This neglect is rather shameful as Miss Magnussen has consistently beaten Miss Lynn in four world championships and two Olympics. . . .

"In contrast to Miss Lynn's artistic conception of skating, Miss Magnussen's approach is athletic . . . and on paper form at least (Karen) should climax her competitive career by winning the world championship. . . ."

Feelings were running high by this time. And the week before the world championships were to begin, I had been asked to take part in a Canadian Broadcasting Corporation television show along with the CBC's Bill Good, Jr., and skating judge Dorothy McLeod, at the close of which there had been the inevitable request for a forecast on the outcome of the ladies' championship.

My answer was, "I believe Karen will win because she has the 'guts' to do so. She will be the one who is better prepared mentally because she is so determined to win." It was a prophecy I'm glad I made. Because it was to tell the story of the 1973 world championships in a nutshell.

13

ON THE THRESHOLD OF SUCCESS

I think it's important to have schools for judges, like those they started in Bratislava. A lot of things were found out that way – like how little some people really knew. It's too bad, really, that they didn't start before now to teach judges all they should know to do a job properly.

So to Bratislava. And what more significant location for an event so full of intrigue and suspense than this Slovakian capital, just a taxi ride from the political "iron curtain," and the bright lights of Harry Lime's Vienna on the other side?

The world championship schedule, drawn up by the Czechoslovak organizing committee with the approval of the International Skating Union, called for the ladies' championship to start first, at 8 a.m. on Tuesday, February 27.

Eight o'clock in the morning! Not for figure skaters the luxury of sleeping late. Invariably, in national and international competition, school figures open the agenda, often before daylight because of the many hours needed to cram these unexciting necessities into the schedule. The more interesting and colorful free-skating events, attracting far larger attendances, are naturally scheduled for later in the day. The figures – brackets, loops, paragraphs, and so on – take place in the morning, when only the most ardent spectators are sprinkled around the huge arenas.

The previous evening, beneath the gorgeous chandeliers in the Slovak Philharmonic Hall in downtown Bratislava, twenty-eight of the thirty girls who had won their way to the world finals through national competition had taken turns to go on stage and draw a number – the order in which they would skate the first of their three figures. Numbers 29 and 30 were removed first, since two of the original thirty entrants, Sonja Balun of Austria and Krisztina Homolya of Hungary, had made late withdrawals.

Karen drew number two – with a wry smile, since most skaters prefer to be drawn nearer the end of the list. Czechoslovak champion Liana Drahova, to a disappointed roar from the packed hall, drew number one. Janet Lynn drew number nine. (The skating order changes around automatically for the second and third figures, and again for the free-skating.)

As the ranking skater, following her silver medal victories in Sapporo and Calgary the previous year and the retirement of gold medallist Trixi Schuba, Karen was also asked to draw the group of compulsory figures that would be

BRIAN KENT, VANCOUVER SUN

25/ *Bulletin board at the North Shore Winter Club provides unusual backdrop as Karen does calisthenics in preparation for the 1972 Winter Olympic Games in Japan.*

26/ Award for the most outstanding female athlete in Canada of 1972 is presented to Karen by Federal Health Minister Marc Lalonde, at reception in Ottawa.

27/ The 1972 Olympic Games victory podium in Sapporo, Japan, when Karen finished second to Austria's Trixi Schuba (center); Janet Lynn placed third.

28/ Tracing figures is an arduous, exacting ritual. Karen and coach Linda Brauckmann study patterns on the ice during figures practice at North Shore Winter Club in preparation for the 1972 world and Olympic championships.

29/ Japanese lady (who said she wanted to 'adopt' Karen)
helps Olympic silver medallist into authentic Japanese costume
for civic reception in Sapporo. In colorful dress, Karen was
the belle of the ball.

30/ C.P. Air pilots John Sparkes (left) and Bob Goldie hoist Karen aloft in triumph, on her return home after winning a silver medal at 1972 Winter Olympic Games.

31

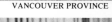

31/ *Congratulations for Karen from Prime Minister Pierre Elliott Trudeau in Ottawa, after silver medal wins in the 1972 Winter Olympics at Sapporo and 1972 world championships in Calgary.*

32/ *Rare are the moments when a star can relax, but Karen managed forty winks after returning home with a silver medal from the 1972 Winter Olympics. She is watched by Alf and Gloria Magnussen, sisters Lori and Judy.*

33/ *Mutual admiration is shown by Karen and another long-time friend, Charles Schulz of 'Peanuts' fame. At 1972 world championships in Calgary, Schulz presented Karen with an original cartoon.*

34

35

PACIFIC STARS AND STRIPES

GORDON SEDAWIE, VANCOUVER PROVINCE

34/ *Janet Lynn (left) and Trixi Schuba (right) helped Karen celebrate twentieth birthday.*

35/ *Dorothy Hamill of the U.S. team and Karen share a joke with a famous admirer—Sammy Davis.*

36/ *Karen with two old friends, Linda Carbonetto, who beat her for the Canadian championship in 1969, and former Canadian men's champion, Jay Humphry.*

KIAPA

37/ Never-ending practice for Karen—this time before mirror at the rink of the Toronto Cricket, Skating and Curling Club, during the summer of 1972.

38/ And didn't this picture cause a sensation? Karen astride the ergometer during maximum-exertion tests at Simon Fraser University. Picture made almost every Canadian daily newspaper, plus many in the U.S.

39/ Brother and sister team of Sandra and Val Bezic, the Canadian pairs champions, are old friends of Karen. Here Karen takes time out from a session at a 1972 summer school in Toronto to chat with the Bezics.

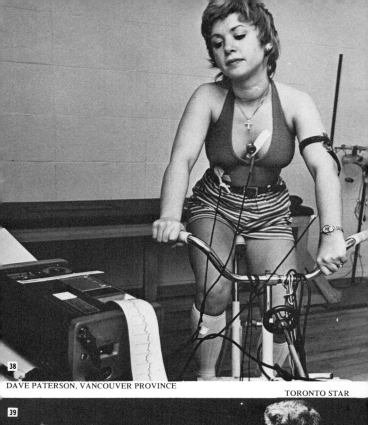

40

41

40/ *Karen caught in mid-air by camera, in demonstration of a fine flying sit-spin after the Canadian championships of 1973.*

41/ *Grace, skill, strength and beauty are all contained in the movements of a skating champion—as evidenced in this picture taken after the Canadian championships.*

42/ *What are those judges up to now? Karen and coach Linda Brauckmann study closely the marks of judges, during competition at the 1973 Canadian championships, when Karen won her fifth national title.*

43/ *One of the duties Karen is always happy to perform. Here, she addresses a United Appeal fund-gathering dinner at Calgary's Hotel Palliser in September 1972, during brief rest from World Championship tour.*

PETER HULBERT, VANCOUVER PROVINCE

JAMES MATHIESON PHOTO, CALGARY

KIYO OF HOLIDAY STUDIO

CANADIAN PRESS PHOTO

44/ *Karen following 1973 Canadian championships is flanked by runner-up Cathy Lee Irwin and bronze medallist, Lynn Nightingale.*

45/ *On their way to the world championships in Bratislava, Cathy Lee Irwin, Toller Cranston and Karen display quite a varied wardrobe.*

46/ *Alf Magnussen and Karen's sisters, Lori and Judy, prepare to say goodbye to Karen and Mrs. Magnussen as they leave for Bratislava and 1973 world championships.*
BILL CUNNINGHAM, VANCOUVER PROVINCE

47/ Karen and Canadian men's champion Toller Cranston center the 14-strong Canadian team, selected at the 1973 Canadian championships to compete in the world championships in Czechoslovakia.

48/ Never idle, Karen finds time to sew patch on jacket as she waits at Toronto International Airport for plane taking the Canadian team to Vienna, where the skaters practiced for the 1973 world championships.

skated, one of three groups of three figures, each comprising the most difficult of the complete repertoire of over forty figures that every world-class competitor must be able to trace. The figures to be skated in competition are drawn just before the event, so that last-minute "cramming" is not possible.

From the hat, that Monday evening in Bratislava, Karen drew the group of figures that she and twenty-seven other contestants would skate. She drew Group Three – right foot. This meant the figures to be skated would be first the right outside counter, next the left backward paragraph loop, and finally the right forward paragraph bracket.

The next morning, wearing a short Black Watch tartan skating dress and white cardigan sweater knotted at the waist, Karen began her campaign for the championship of the world, under the unwavering scrutiny of nine judges.

Judges in international skating competition are selected first by their national associations. Six of the nine come automatically from those countries whose skaters placed highest in the previous world championships – in this case Austria (Trixi Schuba), Canada (Karen Magnussen), the United States (Janet Lynn), Hungary (Susie Almassy), Britain (Jean Scott), and East Germany (Sonja Morgenstern). The other three judges are chosen by lot from the other countries with entries in the event. The three that came out of the hat were Finland, Holland, and Switzerland.

So the nine "members of the jury" assembled to adjudicate the ladies' world championship of 1973 were: Mrs. Helga von Wiecki of East Germany, Mrs. Mary Louise Wright of the United States, Ludwig Gassner of Austria, Mrs. Vera Lynfield of Britain, Mrs. Elisabeth Bon-Meyer of Holland, Mrs. Inkeri Soininen of Finland, Dr. Jakob Biedermann of Switzerland, Mrs. Joan Maclagan of Calgary, Canada, and Mrs. Martha Leces of Hungary. (It will help the reader to remember the judges in that order, since the marks that each awarded, which will be scrutinized later, follow that order, from one to nine.)

With Karen skating early in the order, more people than usual were on hand in Zimny Stadium that raw Tuesday morning, many of them armed with large notepads to record the marks. Some also came equipped with transistorized pocket-computers, to work out their own results and standings before the championship auditors, hidden away in the bowels of the stadium, could produce and verify official results.

Skating marks are as complicated as anything in the world of sport. They are difficult for the layman to understand, more difficult to work out. It is important, for the moment, to remember that the marks themselves are of secondary importance. The order in which each judge places each skater, and a majority system of voting, decide the ultimate victor. Hence the need for those computers!

Each girl would skate the first figure, in the order drawn the previous evening, then the whole process would be repeated, in different order, for the second figure and so on. Before the three figures were completed it would be 6 p.m., the judges would be numb – despite fur coats, hats and boots – from standing (even, on occasion, kneeling) on the ice to examine closely the tracings of the skaters. And twenty-eight young women would be in various stages of shock or exhilaration, depending on their performances and the judges' reaction.

The human computers were busy from the start. For the first figure, the counter, Karen drew these marks from the nine judges (in the order already mentioned):

4.5 4.5 4.5 4.5 4.3 4.2 4.2 4.4 4.3.

Marks are awarded out of a possible 6.0, so these may not appear too good. But it is customary for figures' marks to be considerably lower than those awarded for free-skating (a procedure with which many critics are immediately at odds). Nowhere will you find a 5.8, 5.9, or 6.0 mark for a school figure, though such awards are now commonplace in championship-caliber free-skating.

Trixi Schuba of Austria, generally regarded as

one of the greatest exponents of figures in the history of competitive skating, had been awarded the following nine marks for the first figure in her 1972 world championship victory in Calgary:

4.6 4.7 4.5 4.4 4.7 5.0 5.0 4.3 5.1,

while Karen's marks had been:

4.0 4.3 4.1 3.8 4.2 4.4 4.3 4.1 4.6.

The old saying is true, that figures can be made to prove almost anything. But for those scribbling furiously in Bratislava, the immediate indication was that, while Karen was receiving a sort of guarded approval from the judges, she was not being allowed to open up any sort of margin on the rest of the girls.

Although Karen's first-figure marks were reasonably good – and put her in first place at that stage with six of the nine judges – the fact that the other three judges rated her lower than someone else meant that her lead at the top was not as substantial as had been hoped. Hungary's Mrs. Leces had Switzerland's Karin Iten first, followed by Karen and Janet Lynn; Switzerland's Dr. Biedermann had the Swiss girl first with Janet second and Karen third, while Finland's Mrs. Soininen had Janet first, Miss Iten second and Karen third.

To appreciate the significance, the marks awarded by each judge to the top five girls should be studied:

	Magnussen	Lynn	Iten	Scott	Errath
E. GERM.	4.5	4.3	4.3	4.2	4.2
U.S.	4.5	4.4	4.3	4.2	4.0
AUST.	4.5	4.4	4.3	4.2	4.2
BRIT.	4.5	4.4	4.2	4.3	4.1
HOLL.	4.3	4.2	4.2	4.0	4.0
FIN.	4.2	4.5	4.3	3.9	3.9
SWIT.	4.2	4.4	4.5	3.9	4.0
CAN.	4.4	4.3	4.2	4.1	4.0
HUNG.	4.3	4.2	4.4	4.0	4.1
TOTAL	39.4	39.1	38.7	36.8	36.5

The pattern appeared to be set. Karen's superior figures would keep her in first place, unless there was a technical disaster. But it would be Janet Lynn, not recognized as strong in figures, who would be second, not the Europeans, Scott and Iten, who were generally considered superior.

So it appeared the scene was already being set for a free-skating showdown between the two North Americans, with the world title hanging on the result – and the figures virtually a waste of time.

The tendency to nationalism among judges will also have been noted: The highest mark received by Miss Errath was awarded by the East German judge; the highest mark given to Miss Iten came from the Swiss judge; the highest mark received by Miss Scott was awarded by the British judge;

and the highest mark for Miss Lynn (outside of the marking of Finland's Mrs. Soininen, of which more later) was from the U.S. judge. In contrast, Karen's award of 4.4 by the Canadian judge was exceeded by four of the other eight judges.

The second figure, the tricky back paragraph loop, confirmed suspicions that the judges were determined to keep things tight in the figures and let everything ride on the free-skating. It produced another fine tracing by Karen, clean and precise. This time it earned the first-place nod of all nine judges. But she was still being kept close to her nearest rivals. The loop marks for the five girls:

	Magnussen	Lynn	Scott	Iten	Errat
E. GERM.	4.4	4.2	4.3	4.2	4.2
U.S.	4.4	4.2	4.2	4.1	4.0
AUST.	4.4	4.2	4.2	4.1	4.2
BRIT.	4.5	4.3	4.3	4.2	4.0
HOLL.	4.4	4.2	4.2	4.1	3.9
FIN.	4.5	4.4	4.0	4.1	3.8
SWIT.	4.3	4.0	4.1	4.1	4.0
CAN.	4.5	4.3	4.2	4.2	4.0
HUNG.	4.5	4.3	4.2	4.4	4.3
TOTAL	39.9	38.1	37.7	37.5	36.4

The marks gave Karen a bit more edge, but Janet was still in second place despite a far from convincing loop.

The third figure was the forward paragraph bracket. To her friends and colleagues on the Canadian team this was "Karen's baby," the figure in which she excelled. If anything was going to open the gate for her, this was it.

The paragraph bracket is a difficult figure. The bracket turn is, briefly, a turn on one foot from forward to backward, or vice versa, from one edge to the other (inside to outside or outside to inside) in a manner counter to normal revolution. Complicated to explain, more so to execute!

Karen laid down a beautiful figure, her confident smile expressing satisfaction. The tracing received marks ranging up to 4.7, best in the competition so far.

But what was this? Here were the marks for Janet Lynn, and far from opening up the expected gap for Karen, the judges had pegged the American girl firmly in second place. Mrs. Soininen actually had the two girls reversed, awarding the lowest mark of the nine (4.4) to Karen and the highest mark of the nine (4.5) to Janet.

The markings of the nine judges for the third and final figure went like this:

	Magnussen	Lynn	Iten	Scott	Errat
E. GERM.	4.5	4.3	4.2	4.2	4.1
U.S.	4.4	4.3	4.0	4.1	4.1
AUST.	4.5	4.3	4.3	4.2	4.1
BRIT.	4.6	4.4	4.4	4.3	4.0
HOLL.	4.6	4.3	4.2	4.2	4.0
FIN.	4.4	4.5	4.2	4.1	4.0
SWIT.	4.6	4.3	4.3	4.0	4.0
CAN.	4.7	4.5	4.2	4.3	4.1
HUNG.	4.5	4.4	4.3	4.1	4.1
TOTAL	40.8	39.3	38.1	37.5	36.5

So there it was. When all the arithmetic was complete, the overall picture confirmed the pattern the judges had established from the start. Karen had the lead. But Janet was solidly in second place ahead of the European girls, setting the stage for the free-skating duel and a definite chance for the American girl to win it all.

The overall table for the figures competition is shown below. It includes the total mark from each judge, the order in which each judge placed the top five girls (the ordinal mark) and the total marks and ordinals for each girl:

	Magnussen	Lynn	Iten	Scott	Errath
GERM.	13.40	12.80	12.70	12.70	12.50
	1	2	3T	3T	5
S.	13.30	12.90	12.40	12.50	12.10
	1	2	4	3	6
JST.	13.40	12.90	12.70	12.60	12.50
	1	2	3	4	5
RIT.	13.60	13.10	12.80	12.90	12.10
	1	2	4	3	5T
OLL.	13.30	12.70	12.50	12.40	11.90
	1	2	3	4	5T
N.	13.10	13.40	12.60	12.00	11.70
	2	1	4	6T	8
VIT.	13.10	12.70	12.90	12.00	12.00
	1	3	2	5T	5T
AN.	13.60	13.10	12.60	12.60	12.10
	1	2	3T	3T	5
UNG.	13.30	12.90	13.10	12.30	12.50
	1	3	2	5	4
TAL	120.10	116.50	114.30	112.00	109.40
	10	19	29	38	49.5

" means tied. 3T indicates that the judge had two or more skaters
d for third place.)

The marks themselves provide ample food for
thought, enough subject matter for endless de-
bate. Critics of the present judging system, and
there are many, will draw from them all the am-
munition they need in any future demands for
change. However, all things are relative. The
judging in this world competition was no worse

than in many other national and international competitions. It was, statistically, more consistent than many, though there will, inevitably, be many arguments over the marks awarded.

From the Magnussen, and Canadian, point of view, the end result was what mattered – eight out of nine first-place votes, with Finland's Mrs. Soininen finding herself considerably adrift from her colleagues. (It has not been disclosed before, but two weeks later when Karen and other medal winners visited Helsinki on the post-championship tour of champions, she was sought out by the Finnish lady who offered profuse apologies for her judging performance in Bratislava!)

Outside of Mrs. Soininen's marks, the most intriguing judging decision in the figures competition was the insistence on placing Janet Lynn second on six of the nine judges' cards and first with Mrs. Soininen, despite the U.S. champion's own acknowledged deficiencies in this area. Janet, who had won a competition in figures only twice – once at intermediate level and once, controversially, in the 1970 U.S. championships – had been asked at Bloomington why she had such trouble with school figures. She had replied, candidly, "Well, my legs aren't straight. I'm bow-legged and flat-footed and if I used some of the positions the other skaters try I'd fall over."

The refreshing candor of the American champion had not, apparently, reached the world judges. Only Switzerland's Dr. Biedermann and Hungary's Mrs. Leces placed her lower than second, in both cases behind Switzerland's sixteen-year-old Karin Iten, the figures winner of the 1973 European championships.

Rinkside opinions were strong, and varied, as always. Nationalism runs at least as high in figure-skating as it does in other world events. Considered opinion is more valid, and the following comment is a reasonably unbiased view of the Bratislava figures competition. It comes from the March 1973 issue of the Los Angeles Figure Skating Club's news bulletin, under the by-line of a respected professional coach, Frank Carroll: "The girls skated their figures first, Karen Magnussen of Canada grabbing the lead immediately – she skated three nice figures, not making any obvious errors. Janet Lynn was second, experiencing some difficulty with the paragraph loop, which was badly off axis. Karin Iten was third; this girl has excellent figures, she won the figures in the European championships and won the Grand Prix in France this summer. . . ." (The axis is an imaginary line that divides the figure in two. Both halves are supposed to be symmetrical.)

However, the results were in – the first results of the 1973 world championships – and Canada already had a gold medal. For the first time, the International Skating Union had decided to award three gold medals, three silver medals, and three bronze medals in both the men's and ladies' singles events – small medals for figures and free-skating and the customary large medals for overall victory. For the ladies' school figures, therefore, the gold medal went to Karen, the silver to Janet Lynn, and the bronze to Karin Iten.

They paved the way for the biggest test of all — the free-skating, with the newly introducd two-minute compulsory program scheduled for the following day, Wednesday, February 28, and the climactic four-minute free program on Thursday.

Once again, the forecasters were off and running. Majority opinion still seemed to favor Janet Lynn, whose free-style, it was suggested, would enable her to overtake Karen for the overall title. Not so the Canadians. "As far as I'm concerned that's one gold medal down and two to go," insisted the Canadian team manager, Charlie Dover.

More cautious, but still optimistic, was Mrs. Barbara Graham, the recently appointed Technical Co-ordinator of the Canadian Figure Skating Association, herself a former ISU judge and an international referee. On the bus back to the Carlton Hotel that Tuesday night, Mrs. Graham described Karen's leading margin as "not great, but still substantial," adding the prediction that chances for the overall gold medal were "good, provided Karen can do it when it counts."

That was putting into brief analysis what many had been suggesting all along, that victory would go to the girl best able to stand up to the almost unbearable pressure of being expected to win. Wednesday's short compulsory program was to provide the immediate answer to the question of which girl it would be.

14

ALL THOSE YEARS – AND OVER!

Sometimes I say to myself, out there on the ice –
"God, I'm working so hard. Are they even noticing?"

For most of its history, figure skating has placed the emphasis on just that – skating figures. Until 1968-69, figures counted for 60 per cent of total marks awarded, with free-skating responsible for the other 40 per cent. With the great technical advances made in free-skating, however, and the demands of television audiences throughout the world for more glamor and excitement, the emphasis gradually shifted.

First the ratio was made equal – 50 per cent for figures, 50 per cent for free-skating. Then in 1973 the International Skating Union revised its rules again. From now on there would be a three-part competition in the singles events. Figures would be still further reduced in importance, with skaters required to perform only three figures instead of six, and the figures would count for only 40 per cent of total marks. Free-skating would remain in its present format and count for another 40 per cent. And a new short compulsory free-skating program would be introduced to take care of the remaining 20 per cent.

Basically the new short program was intended to make sure that competitors could not win a world championship without being efficient in all phases of skating. A figures whiz could not, like Trixi Schuba in 1972, pile up a huge margin in that department, then hang on, while more competent free-skaters tried in vain to overcome her massive lead.

Rule books describe the new short program this way:

> A compulsory, connected program with prescribed free-skating elements, to music. The compulsory connected program shall contain the six basic elements listed in one of the three groups set out below . . . this program shall not exceed two minutes duration, but may be less, provided that all the stipulated elements are included. Additional elements are not allowed, but necessary connecting steps are permitted. The music and the succession of the prescribed elements in the compulsory program is the choice of the skater.
>
> A mistake, failure or omission of one of the stipulated elements will not lead to a mathematical deduction of one-sixth of the total mark, but shall be reflected in the marking according to the degree of seriousness of the fault and to the difficulty of the failed element.
>
> Marks will be deducted from technical merit as a result of technical errors, and also

from artistic impression if the harmonious and artistic aspects of the program are involved.

The above-mentioned groups are:

Group 1: (a) Axel Paulsen (b) double Axel Paulsen or double lutz (c) jump combination consisting of two jumps with at least one of the following: double loop, double toe Salchow (double flip), double toe loop, double Salchow, (d) flying camel spin, (e) sit spin with change of foot, (f) straight line step sequence.

Group 2: (a) Axel Paulsen (b) double Axel Paulsen or double lutz (c) jump combination consisting of two jumps with at least one of the following: double loop, double toe Salchow (double flip), double toe loop, double Salchow (d) flying sit spin (e) camel spin with change of foot (f) circular step sequence.

Group 3: (a) Axel Paulsen (b) double Axel Paulsen or double lutz (c) jump combination consisting of two jumps with at least one of the following: double loop, double toe Salchow (double flip), double toe loop, double Salchow (d) flying sit spin changing the foot of landing (e) fast upright spin (f) Serpentine step sequence.

Group 3 was the one selected for the 1973 world ladies' championship.

Again, without delving into a maze of technical detail, the importance placed on jumping is obvious. Each group insists on the Axel Paulsen, plus either the double Axel Paulsen or double lutz. The reason is that the Axel Paulsen, more commonly known as simply "the axel," is the most difficult of the various species of jumps in the skating repertoire, with the lutz close behind. Each, incidentally, is named after its originator, as is the Salchow.

On an axel, the skater takes off from the forward outside edge of the skating foot, turns one-and-a-half times in the air, and lands on the back outside edge of the other foot. On a double axel, the skater makes two-and-a-half revolutions in the air. No one, to my knowledge, has ever done a triple axel, three-and-a-half revolutions, at least in competition.

On a lutz, the skater takes off from the back outside edge of the skating foot, assisted by the toe of the free foot, turns one time with a reversed movement and lands on the back outside edge of the original free foot. A double lutz is two revolutions. A triple lutz is three revolutions, though this is so difficult that only one has ever been landed in world competition – by Canada's Donald Jackson, when he won the world title at Prague in 1962.

So much for the technicalities. No further evidence should be required of the need for hours, days, weeks of continuous practice to reach even a reasonable level of achievement in these complicated and athletic maneuvers.

For each of those competing in the world championships at Bratislava, those hours and weeks mounted up to years of solid effort, so it was surprising to discover that Karen Magnussen, still four weeks from her twenty-first birthday, was the second oldest girl in the competition (to Britain's Jean Scott).

On Wednesday, February 28, 1973, all those years of toil were funneled into one two-minute program, with each girl's skill measured against that of her opponents and against the judges' yardstick of quality.

Karen's short program was as typical of the girl as anything could be – strong, decisive, beautifully controlled all the way, with the six required elements produced in a neat, compact package. It was not the all-out, hell-for-leather, breathtaking style of her earlier years. Far too much at stake here for that. She seemed like a thoroughbred on a tight rein, as though she longed to throw off the shackles that competition demanded, and show everyone what Karen Magnussen could really do, given the chance to let loose.

Control was the key. Karen was in complete command of herself as the elements were attacked and vanquished, one by one. To the sensitive, gentle lyricism of Eduard Lalo's "Scherzo," the Canadian champion moved smoothly into an opening double axel, sure and accurately landed, right into the flying change jump sit spin, confidence bursting from every movement.

Next, a delayed axel, perfect in its timing. And straight into the tough combination, in Karen's case a double lutz-double cherry (toe-loop) so that there was no repetition of jumps already performed. Then the serpentine footwork right across the ice, still with that happy smile indicating the sheer joy of accomplishment. And into the final, fast scratch spin as applause welled up from the packed arena.

A total of one minute and thirty-two seconds had elapsed since the first notes of her music. Scarcely an eye had turned away from the graceful, dynamic figure on the ice during that time. It was a "solid" performance from start to finish. It allowed not one hint of anxiety to the contingent of excited Canadians, feverishly waving a huge flag. It was the kind of performance they had come to expect from their champion – purposeful, determined, no time wasted on unnecessary frivolities or aimless arm-waving, no concession to weakness in the choice of jumps, yet superbly graceful and flowing throughout its short span, with everything made to look comfortable and easy.

Quickly the nine judges (the same nine, necessarily, who adjudicated the figures) jotted down their marking awards and passed them to referee Dr. Josef Dedic of Czechoslovakia for scrutiny.

Two marks are awarded in free-skating – in both the short compulsory program and the long free-skating program. The first is for "technical merit," the second for "artistic impression." The two sections may be described, respectively and roughly, as "what you do" and "how you do it." Karen's marks from the nine judges, again out of a maximum of 6.0, were as follows:

	Technical merit	Artistic impression
E. GERM.	5.8	5.7
U.S.	5.7	5.8
AUST.	5.8	5.8
BRIT.	5.9	5.8
HOLL.	5.8	5.9
FIN.	5.8	5.7
SWIT.	5.8	5.7
CAN.	5.9	5.8
HUNG.	5.7	5.7
TOTAL	52.2	51.9

So there was that same hint from the judges. The marks were good. But they were not unbeatable. The hard core of experts in the stands nudged each other and murmured knowingly, "They're leaving room for Janet!" And so it appeared.

Given the same kind of free-skating marks she had received in the previous world championships in Calgary – all 5.8's and 5.9's with a couple of perfect 6.0's for artistic impression thrown in – Janet could edge into the overall lead right here, with the long free-skating program still to come. It was an anxious moment for Magnussen supporters. And if there was more than the usual amount of "pre-judging" muttering, there did appear to be some justification for the suspicion.

Those who subscribed to the pre-judging theory were, in effect, claiming that while the judges acknowledged the flawlessness of Karen's performance, they had deliberately refrained from awarding "super" marks, because they knew that Janet Lynn had yet to skate, and that the American girl, rightly or wrongly, had sometimes received higher free-skating marks than Karen in recent years. Thus there was still the lingering feeling that the crown was being manufactured to fit Miss Lynn, and that all she needed to do was appear on the ice to collect a bushel of 5.9 and 6.0 marks.

The hypothetical question everyone asked was this: If Janet had not been in the competition, what would Karen's marks have been? To that, there is simply no answer.

In any event, the suspicions were to last for only a few minutes. An analysis of judges' marks must be delayed here to return to the highly charged emotion of the championships. For it was precisely this emotion, and the pressure it placed on the leading contenders, that prevented any pre-judging attempt. In her short compulsory program, Karen had confidently accepted her situation as the hard-pressed leader, and had resisted the pressure magnificently.

Now came Janet. And spectators at rinkside gasped at the difference. Those near the entrance to the rink said the U.S. champion was "trembling like a leaf and white as chalk." Now those who had forecast that the abstract qualities of inner strength and determination held the key to this championship were to be proved right beyond question.

From the beginning of Janet's program, catastrophe appeared inevitable. The opening sit-spin was wobbly with some "traveling." Then came complete disaster. The jump combination was scheduled to be double-axel into double toe loop. But a tumble to the ice on the double axel ruined it and cancelled the combination element entirely. Another fall on the basic double axel near the end of the program nullified that element also. Two of the most important and demanding elements of the required six had not been accomplished. A third had been suspect. What were the judges to do, remembering the instructions of the rule book?

> A mistake, failure or omission of one of the stipulated elements will not lead to a mathematical deduction of one-sixth of the total mark, but shall be reflected in the marking according to the degree of seriousness of the fault and to the difficulty of the failed element.

Since the double axel is by common consent the most difficult of all the double jumps, Janet's failure was considerable. These were the marks awarded by the nine judges, side by side with the marks given to Karen's flawless program:

	Technical merit		Artistic impression	
	Magnussen	Lynn	Magnussen	Lynn
E. GERM.	5.8	5.3	5.7	5.2
U.S.	5.7	5.5	5.8	5.5
AUST.	5.8	5.3	5.8	5.3
BRIT.	5.9	5.4	5.8	5.5
HOLL.	5.8	5.3	5.9	5.4
FIN.	5.8	5.2	5.7	5.3
SWIT.	5.8	5.4	5.7	5.6
CAN.	5.9	5.4	5.8	5.4
HUNG.	5.7	5.5	5.7	5.4
TOTAL	52.2	48.3	51.9	48.6

Even a cursory glance at those figures vindicated those who were demanding judging reforms.

The widest margin given by any judge – to separate a flawless program from another in which at least one-third of the stipulated content was missing – was six-tenths of a point, and that by just one of the nine adjudicators. Two of the nine, the U.S. and Hungarian judges, could separate the programs by only two-tenths of a point for technical merit.

One judge, Switzerland's Dr. Biedermann, incredibly could find only one-tenth of a point difference between the artistic impression of a superbly controlled program and one that contained two inelegant falls.

A glance at the order in which each judge placed the girls (the ordinal figure) is even more of an eye-opener. Dr. Biedermann had Janet tied for fifth place with her compatriot Dorothy Hamill, while Austria's Mrs. von Wiecki had the U.S. champion tied for thirteenth with Switzerland's Karin Iten.

Once again, the opinion of American professional Frank Carroll: "Karen Magnussen skated a very accurate, poised short program, without a slip, but not so Janet – it was disastrous. She fell badly on the double axel combination and did not recover, taking another spill on her basic double axel. . . ."

On such evidence, it is clear that judging reforms are necessary. And it is refreshing to note that the International Skating Union is moving to correct the situation – the first international judges' seminar, ironically, having been held immediately after the world championships at Bratislava. Hopefully, the tendency to judge by reputation will soon be removed.

For the immediate purpose of Canadians in Czechoslovakia, however, the outlook was bright and shining. Nothing but complete disaster could now keep Karen from the world title.

It was not because her closest rival had failed. The key to the competition, so far, was that Karen had *not* failed. In the final analysis of the short program, Karen finished first place with 78.04 points, first on the cards of seven of the nine judges. European champion Christine Errath of East Germany, second with 77.0 points, placed first in the opinion of the other two judges

(significantly the East German and Hungarian).
Dorothy Hamill, who had finished so close to
Janet in the U.S. championships, was third with
76.03. And Lynn Nightingale, the sixteen-year-
old Ottawa girl who had finished third behind
Karen and Cathy Lee Irwin in the Canadian
championships, had shot right into the spotlight
by finishing fourth with 74.46 points – in her
world championship debut!

Janet Lynn, perhaps because of the reluctance
of some judges to believe what they had seen,
wound up no worse than twelfth in the short
program, with 72.65 points.

Official standings combining school figures
results with the short compulsory program – to
give an up-to-the-minute overall picture at that
stage of the event – are released by world championship officials only on a points basis, not on
the more important judges' placements or ordinals. But there were many unofficial scorekeepers
in Bratislava who were anxious to have the complete picture right then. And these human computers quickly produced a list that showed Karen
with a commanding overall lead.

With two-thirds of the event – figures and
short compulsory – completed, the Canadian
champion was first on the cards of all nine
judges. Janet Lynn was still second overall, by
virtue of six second-place votes and three thirds.
Britain's popular Jean Scott was lying third,
Karin Iten fourth, Christine Errath fifth, and
Dorothy Hamill sixth.

Miss Nightingale, despite her fourth-place finish in the short program, was somehow still down in the fifteenth place she had occupied after the school figures. Such are the oddities of skating. (If the reader is not already completely confused by the complex marking system, it might be noted that marks awarded in the short program are multiplied by 0.75 which is the so-called "factor," a mathematical device necessary to make the marks worth 20 per cent of the overall mark, the percentage allocated the short program. Karen's two marks of 5.8 and 5.7 awarded by the first judge, totalled 11.5. Multiplied by 0.75 it produced that judge's final award of 8.62. Similarly, in the long free-skating program, there is a factor of 1.5, by which each judge's mark is multiplied, to produce the 40 per cent of total allocated the long program. This is mentioned here only to satisfy eagle-eyed math enthusiasts. Those involved in figure skating know all about "factors." Those who are not are urged to forget all about them!)

With her overall lead now established, Karen had another twenty-four hours to wait before the final hurdle – a day to be spent, not in celebration, but in still more practice for the climactic event, and in genuine sympathy for her rival. Each time she was asked by fascinated reporters to comment on Janet's calamity, Karen's eyes filled with tears. "I know what it's like," she said over and over again. "It's happened to me before and I know just how she feels. We were in the dressing-room together afterwards and she was terribly upset. I feel so sorry, because you just hate that sort of thing to happen to anybody, even your toughest opponent. You always want them to skate their very best – especially in the world championship."

Among the Canadian contingent there was guarded jubilation. Although Karen appeared to be assured of the overall gold medal, no official was willing to run the risk of placing a jinx on the probability by coming right out and saying so. Thus the corps of Canadian newspaper, radio, and television men, numbering maybe a dozen, had to do it for themselves. One story, filed for Canadian newspapers that Wednesday night said, "It won't be over until the nine judges have had their final fling tonight, but a Magnussen world crown right now appears the safest bet of these 1973 championships."

So a new day dawned – Thursday, March 1, another cold, gusty Bratislava morning. Karen awoke about eight o'clock, breakfasted on cheese, rolls, and tea, and set out for the morning practice session in the unheated, newly enclosed rink adjacent to the main arena. Inevitably there were some problems, mainly because the brief practice time allocated did not allow each girl to have her individual music played for a complete program workout. A draw is normally made to determine which girls will have their records played over the loudspeaker system, and it seemed that one or the other of the Canadians was always being left out. At one such session, when the girls were asked to leave the ice before Lynn Nightingale's music had been played, Karen displayed her authority as senior Canadian member present, and refused to leave until her teammate's music was played and Lynn given a chance to go through her routine.

The rest of the day was a drag. A lot of picture-taking by the usual horde of newspaper and agency photographers and television cameras, the kind of drawn-out sessions that skaters dislike in the midst of competition, and a short time to watch other competitors practice. Then back to the hotel for a rest and "fiddling around with skates to keep my mind occupied."

At 4 p.m. Sandra and Val Bezic, the brother-and-sister Canadian pairs champions, called to suggest a bite to eat. It was a routine gesture. The Canadian team was noted for its closeness and team spirit. The fourteen skaters, with ice-dancing champion Barry Soper as "captain" and spokesman, spent most of their spare time together, while the Canadian girls also formed firm friendships with Jean Scott and Maria McLean, the two Scots with whom they shared a dressing room.

Karen had another good friend and booster in Olympic and world men's champion Ondrej Nepela. Ondrej had stayed with the Magnussens in Vancouver between Olympic and world competitions the previous year (when the world championships were in Calgary), so it was natural that Ondrej, a Bratislava law student, wished to reciprocate when the Canadians were visiting his home town.

The late afternoon meal – cucumber salad, a local beef dish and tea – was a pleasant interlude with the Bezics, but the day itself was long. And Karen had opportunity for another couple of hours rest and to think some more before it was time to locate Mrs. Magnussen and coach Linda Brauckmann and head out once more for Zimny Stadium, about a ten-minute bus ride away.

The final section of the ladies' championship, the four-minute free-skating or "long-free" program, had already started by the time they arrived. Rules of skating competition give those who finish in the top half in school figures the benefit of skating in the last half of the free-skating. A draw is then made among those in the top half to determine the exact order of skating. In the Bratislava free-skating finale, Karen was drawn to skate eighteenth, right behind teammate Lynn Nightingale. Cathy Lee Irwin was drawn twenty-fourth, followed successively by Britain's Jean Scott, and finally, by coincidence, the three American girls, Juli McKinstry, Janet Lynn, and Dorothy Hamill.

All the girls moved up one notch when it was announced that Susanne Altura, due to skate in the number four spot, had withdrawn. Miss Altura's decision left Austria without a representative in the event which that country's Trixi Schuba had won on the two previous occasions. Sonja Balun, the other Austrian entry, had pulled out much earlier; rumor had it that her father, a former Czech national, was afraid for her safety.

So there were now twenty-seven entries, and by the time Karen reached the rink, about a third of them had already skated in front of the sell-out audience. Many of the spectators had arrived long before the scheduled 7:30 p.m. start and had spent the time watching preparations for the event. Radio and television broadcasters, occupying the entire end of the rink at ice-level, chattered unceasingly into their microphones, carrying the color and excitement of the scene around the world.

Johnny Esaw, commentator for the Canadian Television Network (CTV) had his own problems. Waiting to go on the air as the first skaters performed, the harassed Esaw, one eye on the competition, the other on his watch, was doing a frantic mathematical countdown. He could tell that, if the competition continued at its present speed, Karen would have finished her program before his telecast went on the air to Canada.

But it's now no secret that CTV did manage to broadcast Karen's perfomance, that the men in charge of resurfacing the ice took an extraordinarily long time to complete their job on this occasion, and that those same workmen were wearing broad grins and a large assortment of maple leaf pins and crests! A commentator, obviously, is not only concerned with doing his thing in front of the cameras.

Meanwhile, on the ice, the best female skaters in the world, each a champion or medal winner in her own country, were displaying talents it had taken most of their young lives to achieve.

In her dressing-room, Karen Magnussen was fighting the butterflies that fluttered around in her stomach. There was a routine she always followed while waiting to be called to the rink. She describes it this way: "I had about a half-hour before I went on the ice. I did exercises. Went to the bathroom a couple of times – the nerves starting to act up a little. Normally I don't take anything for the nervousness, but on this occasion Lynn [Nightingale] had some glucose, so I took a little of that, but that was all. I think it's all psychological anyway, you just take something because you feel it might, you know, make you skate better or something. I don't think these things have any effect, because I've skated just as well without them.

"Usually Mrs. Brauckmann and I don't talk an awful lot at this time. She will remind me of any problems I've had in the past, to try and remember certain parts where I have to change the tempo, and one or two other specific things that may be small, but very important. For instance, right at the end of my program the music changes and it becomes very fast, the last half-minute or so.

"Sometimes I get carried away a little with what I'm doing and I don't change tempo exactly right, so she will remind me of that. Also to keep my hip in, because I've got (giggle) a loose hip, and if I forget that, my landings go all wonky.

"But I don't like to talk too much, so usually we just run through one or two small things, little reminders. And then I just like to be on my own. I like to go in a corner and not say anything to anybody. I like to get my head all together and start getting in one frame of mind and one channel. I set myself up for what I have to do.

"It's hard to describe a state of mind. A lot depends on what the buildup has been before the competition. I was in a very good frame of mind in Bratislava, though I never was sure what the outcome would be. In past years, when I have skated well, and haven't got as high marks as others, it's been an excruciating thing. I've never been over-confident – anyone who is will be crushed before getting anywhere in this sport.

"Mrs. Brauckmann knows me so well now that there's no need for too much communication at the last minute. When she talks and I start replying with monosyllables like 'uh huh! uh huh!' she knows I've started – a sort of withdrawal. It's an automatic thing. I close off everything else. Then she leaves and just waits for me at the gate to the rink. Even during the warmup we don't say much. I'm hearing what she says and taking it in, but by that time I'm almost completely withdrawn into myself.

"In Bratislava I was not worried at all. Even at the Canadian championships earlier I wasn't a bit worried because I knew I was peaking just right for the world championships. Some, I know, were a bit worried. But I guess I take after my Dad who is a very patient person. This is something only the person involved can understand and appreciate. But it's an exciting thing, to feel inside that you are really ready."

And Karen was ready when the call came at 9.45 p.m. In the warmup session each group is allowed before actual skating performance, she went through her practice meticulously, following a prearranged plan. Each of the jumps, spins and other moves that would be melded into a smooth-flowing, four-minute program were tackled in a businesslike manner. A few more kneebends and toe-touches for final loosening-up, and it was time – time to put it all on the line in the most challenging moment of her life. "She looks ready," whispered those who knew her well. And there was the hint of a prayer in the declaration of confidence.

Then the music blazed forth from the loud-speakers – the first strident notes of the second movement of Serge Rachmaninoff's Symphony No. 2 in E Minor, played by Andre Previn and the London Symphony Orchestra, later to merge into the same composer's Concerto No. 3 in D Minor, as recorded by famed concert pianist Witold Malcuzinski and the Warsaw Symphony. And with the first notes of the music, Karen was off and flying.

From the start it was quickly obvious that there was to be no "backing into" the title. Many had

49/ Russian stag jump—a high, perfectly executed manoeuvre —displayed in London, England, during 1973 personal appearance tour.

TONY DUFFY PHOTO

50

51

*50/ Alf Magnussen talks to his world-champion daughter
by long-distance telephone. Karen was in Paris for personal
appearance show, following her world championship victory.*

*51/ Karen with coach Linda Brauckmann, immediately after
completion of championship-winning routine in Bratislava,
March 1, 1973.*

*52/ On the victory podium at Bratislava, with silver medal-
winner Janet Lynn, and bronze medallist, Christine Errath.*

53/ Among those on hand to welcome Karen at Vancouver International Airport, following her world championship victory at Bratislava, was British Columbia Premier, Dave Barrett.

54/ Flower from her bouquet is presented to a young admirer, one of hundreds who turned out to welcome her home after world championship victory. CBC cameraman Peter Allies, in background, adds to his massive library of Magnussen film.

55/ Almost hidden by the throng. Karen is besieged by North Vancouver youngsters for autographs, during civic reception in her honor, just two hours after arriving home with her world title.

BILL CUNNINGHAM, VANCOUVER PROVINCE

HEALTH AND WELFARE CANADA

HEALTH AND WELFARE CANADA

HEALTH AND WELFARE CANADA

*56/ Karen and coach
Linda Brauckmann (left)
are amused by the words
of Prime Minister Pierre
Trudeau at Ottawa
celebrations honoring the
new world champion.*

*57/ Karen Magnussen
and Linda Brauckmann
combined their talents to
produce a world champion-
ship victory. Picture was
taken in Ottawa, following
their return home from
Bratislava.*

*58/ One of Karen's greatest
boosters over the years
has been Hugh Glynn,
executive manager of the
Canadian Figure Skating
Association. Mr. Glynn
greeted Karen in Ottawa
following the 1973 world
championship victory.*

*59/ Superb picture of
Karen's butterfly jump,
taken in London, England,
during series of exhibition
performances. Despite
complexity of the butterfly
and her horizontal, mid-air
position, Karen still
manages to smile.*

60/ Famed concert pianist Witold Malcuzinski exchanges autographs with Karen during a Vancouver concert. Part of Karen's music for world championship routine was a Malcuzinski recording of a Rachmaninoff concerto.

BRIAN KENT, VANCOUVER SUN

61/ Mountains of mail on the Magnussen dining-room table faced Karen after her world championship victory. This is only part of the flood of letters and telegrams from all over the world.

62/ Greeting Karen at her home following world championship victory was author Jeff Cross, who had covered the Bratislava triumph, then returned home to Vancouver, while Karen went on world Tour of Champions.

63

64

65

63/ Karen is an excellent cook, and has several specialties that she concocts in spare moments off the ice.

64/ At her twenty-first birthday party celebration, April 1973, Karen waves to sellout crowd of 15,711 at Vancouver's Pacific Coliseum. Car was the gift of appreciative fans.

65/ Mrs. Gloria Magnussen wipes away tears of emotion as Karen holds press conference to announce the signing of her Ice Capades contract. Karen's attorney, R. Alan Eagleson, finds it all a huge joke.

66/ Karen takes off on her famed 'Magnussen spiral' during exhibition at 1973 Canadian Figure Skating Bursary Fund dinner in Toronto.

DAVE COOPER, TORONTO SUN

67/ *Karen signs professional contract with Ice Capades. She is watched by Ice Capades president George Eby (right) and lawyer R. Alan Eagleson.*

68/ *During an emotional press conference in North Vancouver, at which she announced her professional contract with Ice Capades, Karen expresses her thanks to everyone who helped her career.*

69/ *Canadian officials were ecstatic when Karen won her world crown—especially John McKay of Chatham, Ontario, president of the Canadian Figure Skating Association.*

70/ Stalwart members of the Laval, Quebec police force provided a personal bodyguard for an entire week when Karen visited that city to take part in a tremendously successful carnival.

71/ Presentation by Mayor Jean Drapeau is made to Karen on behalf of people of Montreal, during exhibition tour of Quebec, following the 1973 world championships.

72/ Champions all! Karen and a long-time friend, Canadian men's champion Toller Cranston, pause for a chat with former hockey great Jean Beliveau of the Montreal Canadiens, in April 1973.

ERIC RATHBORNE FOR B.C. SPORTS HALL OF FAME

73/ *Figure-skating showcase at the British Columbia Sports Hall of Fame is dominated by photograph of Karen. It includes many of the hundreds of trophies, medals and souvenirs of her career.*

74/ *Thoroughly enjoying herself, Karen takes a few steps with youngsters rehearsing for the "Kids on Ice" charity show on behalf of the Cerebral Palsy Fund. Show was held at Vancouver's Pacific Coliseum in 1973.*

ED PRYOR PHOTOGRAPHERS LTD

expected a cautious, careful approach, taking no chances with victory in sight. But there was no such negative thinking. The superbly choreographed program, with all its jumps, spins, and little nuances, was intact – the only compromise with caution being to switch a second double axel into a single axel. The rest was all there, the opening "falling leaf" moves, camel turns, and flying camel with expressive variations of arm movements leading into the first jump, a double flip beautifully executed.

So the four-minute program continued – flying sit spin, double axel, double lutz and into the unique combination of split jumps each way – axel – double loop – butterfly – illusion – and spin.

Then more Magnussen specials: the long, long spiral; the camel spin on a forward outside circle which Karen calls her "747"; the new "waterfall" step, into a double loop; and a new layback made up especially for the championships; a walley jump; another axel; a graceful Ina Bauer spread eagle swerving along the ice, another flying sit spin and then, with the Rachmaninoff music swelling to its climax, the final combination ending wth a perfectly landed double toe loop.

That was it. A superbly controlled program, chock full of skating's most intricate maneuvers, plus a few of her own invention.

And now it was finished. Exhausted by the mental and physical effort, too numb to think of anything except, "Wow, I did it all . . . all those years . . . and it's all over," Karen slumped on the shoulder of her coach, while television cameras whirled and everyone waited for the marks to light up the scoreboard.

After agonizing moments, they came, and there was no need for the announcer to read them. A huge roar greeted these figures as they flashed into view:

For technical merit:
5.8 5.8 5.9 5.9 5.8 5.8 5.9 5.9 5.9.

For artistic impression:
5.9 5.9 5.9 5.9 5.8 5.8 5.9 5.9 5.8.

Arithmetic was unnecessary. Karen had literally skated away from the rest of the field. The nine judges were unanimous. No one else was even close. And Karen was champion of the world.

15

THE AFTERMATH OF VICTORY

It's never really bothered me too much, but I have had to restrict my social life. Now it's exciting to think that I can go out and have a good time. It's sort of new to me, not just something I've been doing since I was thirteen or fourteen. It will be a whole new experience.

As the cheers and applause rolled down from the packed arena, and the huge Canadian flag waved frantically from the upper tier, Karen stood at center ice, motionless, as if a great weight had suddenly been lifted from her shoulders. "I was stunned," she recalled later. "I felt like I had been hit by a two-by-four. But my first conscious thought was of honest-to-gosh relief that it was all over, that I had done it all.

"I had no thought at all that I had won, not right there. I didn't feel it until later, when I was on the podium and receiving the gold medal. I only remember being so happy that I had skated well. You know, it had been forecast by some people that the competition was all over before it started. I had had a fall in the Canadian championships, remember, and it was obvious that a lot of people had written me off. I just wanted, right then, to shove it down their throats.

"I'd never felt like that before, but I remember thinking, there on the ice, that I had finally put it all together and showed them I could do it."

She had, indeed. The marks she received were almost academic. The human computers had figured earlier that it would have taken a series of incredibly low marks to halt her romp to the world title. And none of the nine judges was about to argue with the performance just witnessed. Although there were other competitors still to skate, the crown was hers, unanimously.

For every Canadian in Bratislava, it was a night to howl. The small corps of Canadian press and radio men raced for the nearby press room to file the bulletin, then settle back to write the story they had been itching, for years, to write. First they had to talk to Karen – and here there was a small holdup. International Skating Union rules decree that medalists in all world events must undergo a dope test before the result is official. So the three girls – Karen, silver medalist Janet Lynn, and bronze winner Christine Errath of East Germany – were late arriving for the four-language press conference.

Irrepressible Karen has her own version of the delay: "Well, we had to have this urine test and they insisted on having a lady stand over you in the bathroom, to make sure there was no switching bottles or anything. That sure was something different – you don't know how hard it is to go, with someone standing over you. . . ."

With the tests safely out of the way, Karen reached the press room through the inevitable horde of autograph-seekers. She was immediately introduced to the crowd of newsmen. Almost as if she had been practicing it for days, the English language announcer told the throng: "We would like now to introduce the new ladies' champion of the world – Miss Janet Lynn."

In the roar of laughter and embarrassed confusion that followed, Karen merely blinked a couple of times, half-turned to look at the unfortunate lady, and grinned. She had three gold medals around her neck – one for figures, one for free-skating, and one for the overall world championship, the first-ever clean sweep. She could afford to smile.

Back at the Hotel Carlton, corks popped as Russian champagne flowed. There wasn't much sleep that night for the new champion. Nor for the rest of the week, for that matter. In the whirl of receptions, luncheons and banquets which followed, Karen was the belle of Bratislava. The frantic pace was to continue, in fact, for the next three weeks, while all the champions and medalists visited the main centers of Europe on the regular post-championship "tour of champions."

For Karen it was a pleasant-enough duty – visits to Moscow, Berlin, Paris, Copenhagen, Oslo, all the storybook European capitals. Everywhere, she received a champion's welcome from packed houses.

There were many interesting sidelights – a performance of "Giselle" by the Bolshoi Ballet in Moscow for instance – and gifts galore for all the young skating stars. In Oslo, capital of her father's native Norway, she was introduced as "the champion of the world, Miss Karen Magnussen . . . of Norway."

And finally, home to Canada, where celebrations were even more lavish. A desk-thumping ovation from members of the House of Commons in Ottawa, and a presentation from Prime Minister Pierre Trudeau, whose wife had attended the same North Vancouver school as Karen. "You have shown that the pursuit of excellence is within the reach of everyone of Canada. It's something that is reflected in all of us," said the P.M. Karen was moved to tears.

In Vancouver there was an airport welcome by Premier Dave Barrett and other dignitaries, then a motorcade through downtown streets. Then, two days after her arrival home came the final tribute. A twenty-first birthday party arranged by the Pacific National Exhibition drew a capacity crowd of 15,711 to the Pacific Coliseum.

Tickets at $1 a head were sold out long before the day, the proceeds after expenses ($12,522.76) going into a bursary fund in Karen's name to assist future young skaters. Gloria Magnussen announced later: "The bursary will be administered by a committee composed of Karen, Mario Caravetta (manager of the Pacific Coliseum), Fred Boates, (manager of the North Shore Winter Club), Mrs. Billie Mitchell (vice-president of the C.F.S.A.), lawyer Alan Eagleson, Jeff Cross of the *Vancouver Daily Province*, and myself."

It was, said Karen that night, the best birthday present of all, "because it will make possible the development of promising young skaters who may, one day, bring more skating titles to Canada."

That night was one to remember: massed choirs singing Happy Birthday, pipe bands parading, sparkling show numbers by Canada's top skaters, and gifts galore, topped by a new automobile, the gift of admirers, through local radio station CKNW. Overcome by it all, Karen said simply: "I think I must be the luckiest girl in the world."

So the saga of Karen Magnussen was almost complete, there in the midst of her friends on her twenty-first birthday. Almost, but not quite.

Two months later the North Shore Winter Club staged its annual skating carnival. The star – Karen Magnussen. The production theme – Cinderella. Minutes after the final curtain, president George Eby of the touring Ice Capades Revue announced proudly that his company had just signed Cinderella to the largest contract it had ever offered a skater turning professional, worth some $300,000 for three years.

Karen joined Ice Capades for its opening show of the 1973-1974 season in Duluth, Minnesota, the regular breaking-in center for the company. Before a packed audience in the Duluth Arena, she made her professional bow like a champion.

It was all there – the double axel, the famous Magnussen spiral, the two-way split jumps, the lot. A tough program for a championship competition, even tougher in a restricted rink under the glare of dancing spotlights.

Why would she push herself in such a demanding routine, eight times a week, when the average showgoer would be quite happy with a much less strenuous program? "Well," said Karen Magnussen simply, "these people are paying money to see the world's best. I feel I should skate like the champion."

EPILOGUE

*All British Columbia watched your great
determination to bring your province honor.*

*You are a great example for young British
Columbia. In our province, you became Karen
of British Columbia. Overseas you became
Karen of Canada. Now we are so proud to salute
you as Karen of the world.*

Hon. W. A. C. Bennett.

The telegram from the former Premier of British
Columbia was one of hundreds, scattered around
the Magnussen living room. The large dining
table was piled high with stacks of unopened
letters that summer morning, and more arrived
with each mail delivery.

"I think it's just incredible that all these
people take the time to write," said Karen. "Most
of them are from people I don't even know. And
some of those from school kids are just beautiful."

Gloria Magnussen, the mother-manager, sat at
the table, trying to make some inroads into the
mountain of mail, sorting, tabulating, classifying,
occasionally interrupting the conversation with:
"Just listen to this one. It's from a bunch of kids
in Tokyo. . . ."

"I don't know how I'll ever find time to answer them all," smiled Karen ruefully. "But I do try to answer all the letters that need a reply . . . I guess they won't mind waiting for a little while."

Her voice was tired. The little-girl giggle that had punctuated earlier conversation about the past came through only occasionally. She yawned frequently, each time shaking her head in disbelief at her own weariness.

But each question received the same careful consideration and thoughtful appraisal, though most had been answered a thousand times. What about her rivalry with Janet Lynn? Was it as fierce as some people made out? How did they behave, when they were out of the public gaze?

"We have a fine relationship," said Karen firmly. "We're both competitors, but we're friendly off the ice. There's never been a time when we'd walk past each other without a 'hello.' We'd always talk to each other in the dressing-room and wish each other good luck. You know, she can't help it if all these incidents happen. It's not her fault."

But wasn't there a little bit of knife-work at Bratislava, particularly in the exhibition performances after the championships were all over and both girls were called on to skate again, this time just for pleasure?

The little giggle again, from Karen. "I guess that was just a little upstaging by both of us," she grinned. "Janet did her number, then stayed on the ice for two encores. So when it came my turn, I did my number — and three encores."

It was, in fact, something more than a numerical victory. Mischievously, she had started with a pleasant, easy-paced routine to the tune of "Greensleeves." It brought a polite response from the packed Zimny Stadium audience. Then came the crunch — a whirling, twisting, jumping routine to a series of gusty, foot-stomping Slovak folktunes that had been quietly pre-arranged for just such an occasion as this. It had the Bratislava audience roaring approval. Then, without any music, a demonstration of the famed "Magnussen spiral." And finally, as if to show that she could skate all night if they wanted her to, Karen zipped through a quick succession of five soaring split-jumps. It had exactly the intended effect.

The Magnussen spiral, the two-way split-jumps, the endless series of combination moves she had introduced to the skating scene — would she like to be remembered for these?

"It would be nice to be remembered as someone who improved the concept of skating . . . made it something more than just a series of jumps and spins . . . turned it into a complete artistic presentation."

Karen gestured eloquently. "That's something we've always strived for, Mrs. Brauckmann and I. Each year we tried to introduce something new, to get as much into the program as possible. People like to see something different. You have to give them variety. That was one reason I did that show number with an umbrella, to 'Raindrops.' Something a bit different. That was very popular."

How about this selection of moves? Doesn't it require an awful lot of preparation, apart from the necessary hours of practice on skating technique and the essential work on school figures?

"I think it's the hardest work of all," said Karen. "It takes so many extra hours to get these things perfected. We can have a basic program put together in about an hour, Mrs. Brauckmann and I, maybe even half an hour, but it's the in-between stuff that takes all the time. That's what puts it all together, what dresses it up.

"I remember when I first started with Mrs. Brauckmann, I was including a Russian split jump in my routine. It's different from the scissor-split; in the Russian jump you sort of bring both legs up in front of you. But it's not really a girl's jump – it's a real crotchy kind of thing. Mrs. Brauckmann called me over to the side and said: 'Egad, girl! What are you *doing?*' And right there we switched to the scissor-split . . . one leg in front, the other behind, while facing the way I was going."

What about these jumps? Years ago, even a double jump was a rarity. Now there are triples. Where is it all going?

"I don't think triple jumps are all that important . . . not for the girls," said Karen decidedly. "They're necessary for the boys, all that athletic stuff, but for girls there are so many other things they can do – flying camels, sit-spins and so on. Boys have to do the physical stuff, but I think it's a mistake for the girls to try to copy them. Girls don't want to wind up look-ing like boys.

"Mind you, I imagine triple jumps will soon be a 'must' thing for the girls as well. A lot of the girls do them in practice, though only Sonja Morgenstern has landed one in world competi-tion so far.

"Actually I was doing triples five years ago, a triple Salchow mainly, and for a whole season before Bratislava I worked on a triple loop that I could have put into the split-split combination if it had been needed. However, as it turned out, it wasn't necessary."

Judging jumps must be terribly difficult, don't you think? I hear from all sides that many skat-ers, even in world competition, "cheat" on jumps and don't get penalized for it. Is this true? And what does it mean exactly?

"Well, it is possible to cheat a jump, like a double axel, for instance." Karen twisted around in her chair, went through the slow-motion rou-tine of an imaginary double axel with a frown of concentration.

"On a double axel, you have to take off from the forward outside edge of the skating foot, turn two-and-a-half times in the air, then land on the back outside edge of the original free foot. You can cheat the jump by landing forward instead of backward and completing the final turn while on the ice, instead of in the air. Some people also cheat on the takeoff, starting the turn before the skating leg is up in the air. They get so good at it, it's hard to spot. And you see a lot of it, even as you say, in world competition where skaters get good marks for cheated jumps. It's done so fast that it's difficult to tell unless you're watching very closely.

"I can't cheat a jump," said Karen matter-of-factly. "I either land it properly or I wipe out. It must be the way I'm built, or the way I was taught. One year I even tried to do cheat-jumps, but I found I just couldn't manage them."

Doesn't this mean, then, that there's a lot of room for improvement in the judging of skating? I know it's always been a contentious issue and that judges bear the brunt of a lot of criticism. Is it all justified?

"Some of it is, for sure," said Karen firmly. "You know as well as I do that skating is a very political thing. You've written lots of stories about the weird things that go on, both before and during competition. The human element is there, and I guess it's something you have to live with.

"But I honestly think it's getting better. One of the best things to happen was the international judging school that was held right after the world competition in Bratislava. I hope they're going to have a lot more. They might embarrass a lot of people, but it will be worth it."

"Show Jeff your mink coat," called Gloria from the kitchen.

"Oh, yeah, did you hear about that?" sparkled Karen. She jumped up, ran to the bedroom, and came back wearing a gorgeous, full-length black mink.

"When I did an exhibition show at Laval, Quebec, one of the people connected with the show, a Mr. Irving Camlot, took me down to his store – he's co-proprietor of a big company that has made fur coats for Margaret Trudeau and lots of other people. He told me to pick out whatever I wanted. I couldn't believe it. Isn't it super? It's Canadian Majestic – it's a trench coat, with military epaulettes, and velvet pockets, even has my name sewn into the lining. And spelled right, too!"

Gloria brought in more coffee, plus some goodies Karen herself had baked the day before. But now she wrinkled up her nose at them.

"Have to watch that stuff," she sighed, glancing down at her waist and giving herself a reassuring pat. "I was usually about 115 pounds in competition, but now I'm down to about 110, and I'm going to lose a little more. Have you seen those Ice-Capades girls? They're all so slim. Guess they don't have any competition muscles. But I'm working at it – special exercises, strict diet, that kind of thing. And it seems to be a success."

What about show-business? You've said that it's going to be fun, but still hard work, what with eight and sometimes nine shows a week. You are also the first one ever to have to skate with both East and West companies of the show, aren't you? That means a completely different life style. Is that your future? Or will there be something else?

"I think maybe three years in the show," said Karen. "I don't know, but that may be enough."

And then?

"I'd like to do some teaching. I like kids. You get a lot of satisfaction out of working with them. And I'd like to put back into skating some of the things I've taken out."

I guess there'll be no more competition skating, eh? There is talk that Dick Button is proposing a so-called professional championship to be held in Japan at Christmas, though scuttlebutt is that it is being engineered just to get a world title of some kind for Janet, so she can be billed as a "world champion" in her professional promotion.

"Yeah, I've heard about that one," grimaced Karen. "There have been overtures made, to me and some of the other kids. But there's no point. It takes a whole different setup to practice for a competition. And you can't do it while you're in a show. Besides, there'd be nothing to gain. I don't think anyone is taking it very seriously."

One thing is clear. You now have a totally different way of life from the past. Does it stack up the way you expected it would?

Karen glowed. "I think it's just the most exciting thing of all," she answered. "I can look back and think that I've done all the things I set out to do. I achieved my ambition in skating. I finished my first year at university and I can go back and complete my studies later on. I've got friends all over the world. I've been inducted into the B.C. and Canadian Sports Halls of Fame and honored by the Order of Canada award. I'm financially able to do things for Mom and Dad and my sisters, in return for all the things they've done for me and given up for me. And there's nothing, anywhere, that I would ever be ashamed of."

I guess there's only one thing left, isn't there? What about marriage? You're young, attractive, financially independent . . . could we say Canada's most eligible bachelor girl? I guess there must be someone waiting in the wings?

"Not a soul," chuckled Karen Magnussen. "I'm as happy and as free as a bird."

And come to think of it, that was perhaps the most accurate analogy she could have made.

APPENDIX 1

GLOSSARY OF SKATING TERMS

axel:
More correctly the Axel Paulsen jump, named for its originator. To do an axel, the skater must take off from the forward outside edge of the skating foot, turn in the air one and one-half revolutions, then land on the back outside edge of the original free foot. A double axel is two and one-half revolutions. A triple axel would be three and one-half revolutions in the air. The axel is generally considered to be the most difficult of the jumps.

butterfly:
Also known as the Arabian Cartwheel. It is usually done from an inside edge, using the skating foot as a lever and thrusting the free leg back and up. Then the skater takes off with both legs behind and both arms thrust out forward, assuming a position in mid-air with the body horizontal to the ice.

camel spin:
A one-foot spin with the body and free leg in a horizontal position.

cherry: See *toe loop.*

flip jump:
A toe jump in which the skater takes off from the back inside edge of the skating foot, assisted by the toe pick of the free foot. There is one complete turn in the air, then the landing is on the back outside edge of the original free foot. A double flip is two revolutions in the air, a triple flip is three revolutions. The jump is also sometimes called "a toe Salchow."

illusion:
A type of spin performed either right or left. The illusion is done on the turn. Normally the free leg goes forward as the same arm follows its direction. Then the trunk bends forward and the free leg is drawn back with the arm reaching downwards and pointing towards the ice. Sometimes done several times in quick succession.

loop:
Or loop-jump, to avoid confusion with the compulsory figure "loop." The skater takes off from the back outside edge of the skating foot, turns one time in the air and lands on the back outside edge of the take-off foot. A double loop is two revolutions in the air, a triple loop three revolutions.

lutz:
The lutz is considered next in difficulty to the

axel. The skater takes off from the back outside edge of the skating foot assisted by the toe pick of the free foot, turns with a reversed movement one revolution in the air, then lands on the outside edge of the original free foot. A double lutz is two revolutions in the air. A triple lutz is three revolutions.

ordinals:

The judges' placement of a skater in competition i.e. one for first place, two for second, and so on. Thus if a skater has the first-place vote of nine judges, he has nine ordinals. And the lowest total is, of course, best.

patch:

A rectangular section of the ice rink on which school or compulsory figures are practiced.

pivot:

A move in which the skater makes a small circle on one foot while the toe of the other foot is held stationary on the ice behind him.

Salchow:

Another jump named after its originator, in this case Ulrich Salchow (pronounced Sal-cow). The skater takes off from the back inside edge of the skating foot, makes one revolution in the air and lands on the back outside edge of the original free foot. A double Salchow is two revolutions in the air and a triple Salchow three revolutions.

Generally regarded as one of the easiest multi-revolution jumps.

spins:
A term covering a variety of free-skating moves – sit-spins, camel-spins, cross-foot spins, flying sit-spins etc. In all spins, the skater's body rotates while remaining in one spot on the ice.

spiral:
A one-foot glide, with the body and free leg held in a horizontal position. The Magnussen spiral is a change-direction move which takes place during the glide. It is achieved by bringing the free foot forward, then moving the free foot in a 90-degree turn so the skater is facing a direction at right angles to the original direction. It requires great control and strong back muscles.

split jumps:
The scissor split is done, as its name implies, like a pair of scissors, with the skater facing the direction of travel, in a horizontal position with one leg stretched out in front, and the other leg behind the skater. The Russian split copies the well-known Cossack split, the legs spread wide in the same direction as the skater is facing.

spread eagle:
A two-foot glide with both feet on the same edge, inside or outside, with the heels pointing towards each other.

toe loop:
A jump in which the toe pick of the free foot is used on the takeoff, to assist in gaining height and body rotation. Also known as a "cherry." A double toe loop is two revolutions in the air, a triple toe loop three revolutions.

APPENDIX 2

*(The world championship for men began
in 1896)*

1906 Madge Syers-Cave (Britain)
1907 Madge Syers-Cave (Britain)
1908 Lily Kronberger (Hungary)
1909 Lily Kronberger (Hungary)
1910 Lily Kronberger (Hungary)
1911 Lily Kronberger (Hungary)
1912 Opika von Meray Horvath (Hungary)
1913 Opika von Meray Horvath (Hungary)
1914 Opika von Meray Horvath (Hungary)
1915-1921 No championships held
1922 Herma Plank-Szabo (Austria)
1923 Herma Plank-Szabo (Austria)
1924 Herma Plank-Szabo (Austria)
1925 Herma Jaross-Szabo (Austria)
1926 Herma Jaross-Szabo (Austria)
1927 Sonja Henie (Norway)
1928 Sonja Henie (Norway)
1929 Sonja Henie (Norway)
1930 Sonja Henie (Norway)
1931 Sonja Henie (Norway)

1932 Sonja Henie (Norway)
1933 Sonja Henie (Norway)
1934 Sonja Henie (Norway)
1935 Sonja Henie (Norway)
1936 Sonja Henie (Norway)
1937 Cecelia Colledge (Britain)
1938 Megan Taylor (Britain)
1939 Megan Taylor (Britain)
1940-1946 No championships held
1947 Barbara Ann Scott (Canada)
1948 Barbara Ann Scott (Canada)
1949 Aja Vrzanova (Czechoslovakia)
1950 Aja Vrzanova (Czechoslovakia)
1951 Jeanette Altwegg (Britain)
1952 Jacqueline de Bief (France)
1953 Tenley Albright (U.S.A.)
1954 Gundi Busch (Germany)
1955 Tenley Albright (U.S.A.)
1956 Carol Heiss (U.S.A.)
1957 Carol Heiss (U.S.A.)
1958 Carol Heiss (U.S.A.)
1959 Carol Heiss (U.S.A.)
1960 Carol Heiss (U.S.A.)
1961 Championships cancelled following air crash which took the lives of the entire U.S. team
1962 Sjoukje Dijkstra (Netherlands)
1963 Sjoukje Dijkstra (Netherlands)
1964 Sjoukje Dijkstra (Netherlands)
1965 Petra Burka (Canada)
1966 Peggy Fleming (U.S.A.)
1967 Peggy Fleming (U.S.A.)

1968 Peggy Fleming (U.S.A.)
1969 Gabrielle Seyfert (East Germany)
1970 Gabrielle Seyfert (East Germany)
1971 Trixi Schuba (Austria)
1972 Trixi Schuba (Austria)
1973 Karen Magnussen (Canada)

APPENDIX 3

LADIES' FIGURE-SKATING CHAMPIONS OF CANADA

Canadian Figure Skating Association records date back to 1905, though historical records indicate that national championships had actually been held in the latter half of the 19th century.

1905 Anne L. Ewan
1906 Aimee Haycock
1907 No competition. Minto Skating Club, Ottawa, burned down.
1908 Aimee Haycock
1910 Iris Mudge
1911 Lady Evelyn Grey
1912 Eleanor Kingsford
1913 Eleanor Kingsford
1914 Muriel Maunsell
1915-1919 No competitions held
1920 Jeanne Chevalier
1921 Jeanne Chevalier
1922 Dorothy Jenkins
1923 Dorothy Jenkins
1924 Constance Wilson
1925 Cecil Smith
1926 Cecil Smith
1927 Constance Wilson

1928 Margot Barclay
1929 Constance Wilson
1930 Constance Wilson
1931 Constance Wilson Samuel
1932 Constance Wilson Samuel
1933 Constance Wilson Samuel
1934 Constance Wilson Samuel
1935 Constance Wilson Samuel
1936 Eleanor O'Meara
1937 Dorothy Caley
1938 Eleanor O'Meara
1939 Mary Rose Thacker
1940 Norah McCarthy
1941 Mary Rose Thacker
1942 Mary Rose Thacker
1943 No senior championship
1944 Barbara Ann Scott
1945 Barbara Ann Scott
1946 Barbara Ann Scott
1947 Marilyn Ruth Take
1948 Barbara Ann Scott
1949 Suzanne Morrow
1950 Suzanne Morrow
1951 Suzanne Morrow
1952 Marlene Smith
1953 Barbara Gratton
1954 Barbara Gratton
1955 Carole Jane Pachl
1956 Carole Jane Pachl
1957 Carole Jane Pachl
1958 Margaret Crosland
1959 Margaret Crosland

1960 Wendy Griner
1961 Wendy Griner
1962 Wendy Griner
1963 Wendy Griner
1964 Petra Burka
1965 Petra Burka
1966 Petra Burka
1967 Valerie Jones
1968 Karen Magnussen
1969 Linda Carbonetto
1970 Karen Magnussen
1971 Karen Magnussen
1972 Karen Magnussen
1973 Karen Magnussen

APPENDIX 4

KAREN MAGNUSSEN
ACCOMPLISHMENTS TO DATE

Major National, Regional, Sectional,
Invitational Competitions

1959	Kerrisdale Juvenile Free Skating	1st
1961	B.C. Coast (Victoria) Novice Ladies	1st
1962	B.C. Section (Vancouver) Novice Ladies	2nd
1962	B.C. Coast (Vancouver) Junior Ladies	1st
1963	B.C. Section (Prince George) Junior Ladies	1st
1963	North Shore Winter Club Competition Junior Ladies	1st
1964	B.C. Invitationals (Victoria) Most Outstanding Performance	1st
1964	B.C. Coast (North Vancouver) Senior Ladies	1st
1964	B.C. Coast Free-Skating	1st
1965	B.C. Section (North Vancouver) Senior Ladies	1st
1965	Canadian Junior Ladies Champion (Calgary)	1st

1965	B.C. Invitationals Silver (Victoria)	1st
1965	B.C. Invitationals Gold	2nd
1965	B.C. Coast Free-Skating	1st
1966	Senior Canadians (Peterborough) (2nd to Petra Burka, then World Champion, in Free-Skating)	4th
1967	Senior Canadians (Toronto)	2nd
1968	Senior Canadians (Vancouver)	1st
1969	Senior Canadians (Toronto)	2nd
1970	Senior Canadians (Edmonton)	1st
1971	Senior Canadians (Winnipeg)	1st
1972	Senior Canadians (London)	1st
1973	Senior Canadians (Vancouver)	1st

International Placings

1967	North American Senior Ladies	4th
1967	World's (Vienna) (7th Free-Skating)	12th
1968	Olympics (Grenoble) (4th Free-Skating)	7th
1968	World's (Geneva) (4th Free-Skating)	7th
1969	North American (1st Figures)	2nd
1969	World's (Colorado) (Forced to withdraw due to stress fractures to legs)	
1970	World's (Yugoslavia)	4th
1971	North American Senior Ladies Champion	1st
1971	World's (Lyon)	3rd

1972	Olympics (Sapporo)	2nd
	(Silver Medalist)	
1972	World's (Calgary)	2nd
	(Silver Medalist)	
1973	World's – Ladies Champion	1st
	(Winner of three gold medals)	

MS-1973 BRATISLAVA

vypoctove stredisko **tesla**
zeny
celkove vysledky

computing centre **tesla**
ladies figure skating
final results

kon. fin.	— position — p c	k s	v f	k+v s+f	meno name	stat nat.	— total — umist. ordinals	body points
1	1	1	2	1	magnussen karen	cnd	9,0	356,39
2	2	12	1	3	lynn janet	us	18,0	347,85
3	5	2	5	4	errath christine	ddr	31,0	340,90
4	8	3	4	2	hamill dorothy	us	35,0	337,93
5	4	10	11	10	scott jean	gb	47,0	332,10
6	3	14	14	14	iten karin	ch	60,0	329,08
7	9	9	6	6	drahova liana	cs	69,0	327,53
8	10	5	7	7	morgenstern sonja	ddr	76,0	326,53
9	12	7	9	9	mc kinstry juli	us	91,0	323,26
10	15	4	3	5	nightingale lynn	cnd	78,0	325,61
11	7	11	13	13	mc lean maria	gb	96,0	322,68
12	11	13	10	11	irwin cathy lee	cnd	108,0	320,95
13	14	6	8	8	schanderl gerti	brd	114,0	319,69
14	13	8	12	12	potzsch anett	ddr	125,0	316,21
15	6	15	16	16	de leeuw dianne	nl	123,0	316,11
16	23	16	15	15	sanaya marina	urs	149,0	296,67
17	18	23	17	17	watanabe emi	jpn	154,0	294,35
18	16	18	22	20	bierre marie-claude	f	171,0	288,34
19	19	19	19	19	frosio cinzia	i	175,0	287,45
20	21	17	18	18	oeberg liselotte	s	177,0	285,55
21	20	20	21	22	burley sharon	aus	178,0	286,58
22	27	22	20	21	koskinen hannele	sf	204,0	275,77
23	26	21	23	23	dudek grazyna	pl	201,0	276,57
24	25	26	24	25	gazvoda helena	yu	220,0	268,04
25	17	28	27	27	chang myung-su	kor	227,0	264,92
26	24	27	26	26	tverran bente	n	235,0	261,03
27	28	24	25	24	eros agnes	h	231,0	262,58

— sutaz nedokoncili — did not finish —

altura susanne   a

hlavny rozhodca:
referee:

dr. josef dedic

asistent hlavneho rozhodcu:
assistant referee:

dr. oskar madl